CONTENTS

ACKNOWLEDGEMENTS

The authors and publishers would like to thank the following people and organisations for permission to reproduce photographs and other material:

CACHE for the MCQ answer sheet, 1996 CCE Integrated Assignment and CCE Practice Evidence Record;

Irene Tipping for the photographs in Spreads 23, 26, 28, 34, 37, 41;

Ron Adams for the top photograph on Spread 22;

Jill Tallack and Sally Neaum for the bottom photograph on Spread 22;

Suzanne Scrivens for her photograph on Spread 24;

The children of Sporle Playgroup for their drawings on Spread 22;

Bubbles/Pauline Cutler for the cover photograph.

Thanks are also due to Elaine Peel for her valued support.

INTRODUCTION

How to use this book

This book contains information related to all aspects of the CACHE Certificate in Child Care and Education (CCE) and the National Vocational Qualification (NVQ) in Child Care and Education at Level 2. As well as providing the basic theoretical information that child care students need to know, it offers guidance on the production and presentation of essential written evidence and coursework.

The book is intended as a useful source of information for revision purposes and to help candidates in the acquisition of underpinning knowledge for vocational awards in child care and education.

Part 1: Key Concepts in Child Care and Education

The first part of the book is divided into three chapters corresponding to the Health, Play and Social Studies components of the CCE and NVQ 2. Each chapter is presented in a series of spreads which contain important information in an interesting and accessible format.

At the end of each spread a set of questions is provided to help you check your knowledge and understanding. You are recommended to put these answers in writing, as a means of reinforcing your understanding and to generate evidence of your knowledge to include in your portfolio. A set of key words is included at the end of each chapter in this section. These words and phrases are important, so if you cannot remember their meaning, go back through the chapter to find out.

Part 2: Course Assessment

The information given in **Part 2** provides helpful guidance about the other assessed areas of the CCE (the longitudinal assignment and portfolio of evidence), and advice on generating and organising evidence for NVQ 2. Chapters 4 and 5, which cover writing an assignment and portfolio building, are essential reading for all child care students at every level. They contain straightforward information about documentation and presentation, and describe the logical framework for producing the necessary evidence at the required standard.

Chapters 6 and 7 deal specifically with multiple choice questions (MCQs). Chapter 6 provides insight and practical help with answering

MCQs, giving some useful tips and worked examples, including a specimen answer sheet. Chapter 7 consists of three MCQ papers, each containing 40 questions covering a range of questions related to the syllabus for the CACHE Certificate in Child Care and Education. Used correctly, these should be a valuable revision tool. Time yourself accurately, read the questions carefully, insert your answers on the sheet provided and then check your answers with the correct solutions provided in Appendix D at the end of the book. This will reassure you and highlight areas that need more revision!

Appendices
Appendix A consists of a series of questions linked to the underpinning knowledge and understanding required for NVQ2. Each element is identified and questions are linked to specific areas. Many of the answers to these questions can be found in Part 1 of the book, and candidates are referred to the relevant spread for each task. Tick boxes are included so that you can keep an accurate record of your progress and easily identify gaps in your knowledge evidence.

These answers will supplement observed evidence by your supervisor or assessor and are a useful way of generating evidence of underpinning knowledge to include in your portfolio for assessment.

Finally, the book contains a Glossary *(Appendix B)*, a list of suggestions for Further Reading *(Appendix C)* and the answers to the Sample Multiple Choice Papers in Chapter 7 *(Appendix D)*.

We very much hope it will help you in achieving a child care award.

Marian Beaver
Jo Brewster
Anne Keene

STUDY MATRIX FOR DNN AND CCE MODULES

The grid below shows how the spreads in Part 1 of this book relate to Diploma in Nursery Nursing (DNN) and Certificate in Child Care and Education (CCE) modules. For links to NVQ 2 see Appendix A, page 157.

SPREAD	DNN MODULE	CCE MODULE
1	D, G & M	2
2	D	3
3	D & G	3
4	D	3
5	N	3
6	D	3
7	E	4
8	E	4
9	E	4
10	E	4
11	D & E	4
12	D & E	4
13	K	5
14	K	5
15	K	5
16	K	5
17	M	6
18	M	6
19	M	6
20	M	6
21	D	2
22	D	2
23	D	2
24	H & I	7 & 8
25	H & I	7 & 8
26	H & I	7 & 8
27	H & I	7 & 8
28	H & I	7 & 8
29	E & H	7 & 8
30	C	1

Study Matrix *Contd.*

SPREAD	DNN MODULE	CCE MODULE
31	C	1
32	C	1
33	F	9
34	F	9
35	F	9
36	F & J	9
37	J	11
38	J	11
39	J	11
40	J	11
41	F	10
42	F	10
43	Q	12
44	Q	12
45	Q	12
46	Q	12
47	Q	12

PART 1
Key Concepts in Child Care and Education

1 *HEALTH*

This chapter concentrates on important aspects of keeping children safe and healthy, stimulating their physical development, recognising illness and meeting all their physical needs. These physical requirements – warmth, food, shelter, fresh air and sunlight, safety, opportunity to exercise and develop new skills, rest and sleep, a hygienic environment, protection from infection, access to medical services and immunisation – are all vital for children to enable them to progress and achieve their potential in all developmental areas.

All students of child care, at every level, must be able to show their competence in providing a healthy environment for the children in their care and in keeping them safe. Knowledge of practical First Aid and the importance of recording and reporting injuries and hazards is necessary in case accidents do happen. As future child care professionals, students need to know the average stages of physical development so that any deviations can be detected at an early stage and other professionals involved. This knowledge will also equip child care workers to stimulate children in an interesting and challenging way.

Caring for children includes equipping them to become independent and take some responsibility for themselves, encouraging them to enjoy and participate in caring routines. Providing a balanced diet relies on carers knowing what foods children need to grow strong and healthy, and how to prepare them. It also involves an awareness of special diets, allergies and cultural dietary variations.

Being able to detect early signs of illness and understand the significance of different signs and symptoms, knowing where to seek help for children who are unwell and understanding the effects of illness on behaviour and development – all these are necessary to enable the provision of care for the whole child. This chapter will provide a foundation for caring for all children's physical needs.

Preventive Health

Child care workers have a responsibility to the children in their care to keep them well by preventing accidents and minimising the risk of infection and illness.

Understanding how diseases are spread and how to reduce the risks of cross-infection is essential if children are to be kept safe and healthy.

Health professionals conduct regular health checks on children

PERSONAL HYGIENE

Keeping high standards of personal hygiene is important for several reasons:

- It directly prevents the spread of infection
- It provides a positive example for children

Child care workers should wash their hands often throughout the day, especially after going to the toilet, cleaning up after children's accidents, before handling food etc. It is more difficult to keep long nails clean, so nails should be kept short to prevent infection and to avoid injuring children. Nail varnish should not be worn – bacteria grows where varnish is chipped. Hair should be kept clean and tied back.

IMMUNISATION IN EARLY CHILDHOOD

Because babies and children are very vulnerable to infection, especially before they have developed their own antibodies, the following schedule of childhood immunisations is given to children with their parents' consent.

Immunisation protects children from serious diseases and prevents them passing on diseases to others. Children who have not been immunised are at more risk.

AGE	IMMUNISATION	METHOD
2 months	HIB (meningitis) Diphtheria, whooping cough, tetanus Polio	1 injection 1 injection By mouth
3 months	HIB (meningitis) Diphtheria, whooping cough, tetanus Polio	1 injection 1 injection By mouth
4 months	HIB (meningitis) Diphtheria, whooping cough, tetanus Polio	1 injection 1 injection By mouth
12–15 months	Measles, mumps, rubella (MMR)	1 injection
3–5 years pre-school booster	Diphtheria, tetanus, polio Polio	1 injection By mouth

HOW DISEASES ARE SPREAD

- Droplets in the air breathed out from the nose/mouth, e.g. colds, 'flu, measles, mumps and whooping cough.
- Touching existing wounds, rashes or objects used by somebody with an infection, e.g impetigo and athlete's foot. Infection can also enter the body through an open wound, e.g. a cut or scratch.
- Food may carry diseases if it is not fresh, has been stored incorrectly, contaminated by dirty hands or prepared in an unclean area.

- Animals can spread disease if they are allowed to contaminate food or water. Contact with dog and/or cat faeces can cause disease, e.g. toxoplasmosis. Terrapins carry salmonella and are a particular risk if kept as pets at home or school.
- Blood and other body fluids can cause disease if they enter through broken skin. Human Immunopathic Virus (HIV) and hepatitis may be spread this way.

CROSS-INFECTION

Children are extremely vulnerable to infection. Infection can spread very quickly in a child care establishment, especially if hygiene standards are allowed to fall. Basic workplace routines can prevent diseases being spread if they are carried out efficiently and regularly:

- Hand washing is the single most effective means of preventing the spread of infection.
- Avoid overcrowding. The Children Act 1989 lays down strict guidelines on how much floor space is required by children within each age group.
- Damp dust regularly.
- Use cloths and mops only in their designated areas, e.g. floor mops for the toilet area or playroom only.
- Discourage parents from bringing children who are unwell.
- Disinfect toys and play equipment regularly.
- Ensure that the class pet is clean and well

cared for, with regular feeding, cleaning of the cage/tank,changes of bedding etc.
- Regularly check and clean the toilet/bathroom areas.
- Clean up spills and accidents immediately.
- Wear gloves when administering First Aid or cleaning up body fluids (blood, urine).
- Wear gloves for changing nappies.
- Use disposable nappies.
- Ensure adequate ventilation by opening windows to increase oxygen levels.
- Provide regular opportunities for outdoor play.
- Check the outdoor play area for animal excrement and other hazards.
- Use paper towels and tissues with covered bins for their disposal.
- Ensure food is prepared in a separate area.
- Wash and sieve sand.

SCREENING

Children should have regular health checks to ensure that they are developing within normal limits. Every infant and nursery school is attended by a community paediatrician and a

school nurse who performs routine checks on all the children. Children with problems may be referred to the school medical service for review between the usual health appraisals.

Keeping Children Safe

Young children are totally dependent on their carers for protection and survival. By being aware of their stage of development and anticipating risks and dangers that are associated with it, carers can help to create a safe environment and prevent accidents from occurring.

PROVIDING A SAFE ENVIRONMENT

Accidents are the most common cause of death in toddlers and young children. Children are at particular risk because of their stage of development. The supervision they require depends upon their age and the type of activity they are involved in. Every year about 3 million children go to hospital with accidental injuries – 200,000 as the result of accidents at school. Most accidents could be prevented and most accidents occur at home.

AREA	RISK	PREVENTION
Kitchen	Burns and scalds Poisoning Cuts Choking	Cooker guard, coiled electrical flexes Locked storage of medicines and cleaning chemicals Knives stored out of children's reach Toughened safety glass in doors and windows Safety gate Removing small objects from babies' reach, appropriate food for the age of the child
Lounge	Fire	Fireguard
Hallway/stairs	Falls	Safety gates at the foot and top of stairways
Bathroom	Drowning, burns and scalds Poisoning	Put cold water into the bath first. Never leave a child unattended in the bath. Store medicines/drugs/toiletries in a lockable, wall-mounted cabinet.
Bedrooms and upstairs rooms	Falls	Window locks Keep furniture away from the window to avoid climbing. Do not use bunk-beds for children under seven.
Garden	Falls Drowning Electrocution	Soft surfaces under climbing equipment Ladders stored safely Garden pools/ponds fenced off Teaching children to swim Children supervised during outdoor play Circuit breaker for electrical equipment e.g. lawn mowers
Garage/shed	Poisoning	Locked storage of garden/workshop chemicals

OUTDOOR SAFETY

Play areas

Children in play areas should be supervised by a responsible 'watchful' adult during outdoor play who will:

- Encourage co-operative play
- Discourage aggression
- Ensure climbing equipment is sited on a suitable soft-landing surface with space around it
- Lock all external gates and ensure that children cannot leave the play area unsupervised
- Remove potential hazards, e.g. broken equipment, sharp edges, dangerous litter
- Ensure that play equipment is appropriate for the age-group
- Allow children to return to indoor play area at will
- Provide areas for alternative play, e.g. wheeled toys, ball play, obstacle courses etc.

Road safety

Children are at risk on the road both as pedestrians and passengers in motor vehicles. Child care workers can help to ensure their safety by:

- Setting a good example when crossing roads
- Discouraging parents from allowing children under eight years to cross roads alone
- Only allowing children to leave with a responsible adult who is known to them
- Ensuring the adult/child ratio is within the prescribed limit when on trips and visits
- Having a crossing patrol outside schools
- Talking to children about road safety and teaching them the Green Cross Code. The TUFTY Club may generate interest in road safety for young children.
- Discouraging children from using roads and pavements as play areas.

WORKPLACE SAFETY POLICIES AND PROCEDURES

Most establishments have clear safety rules for children's conduct which make it clear what is expected of them and encourage children to behave in a sensible and responsible manner, e.g. walking and not running along corridors, keeping to the left on corridors and stairs, not shouting, fighting or bullying etc.

Stringent safety precautions are also required, e.g. space to move around the building and classrooms, doors with safety catches, non-slip surfaces, safety glass etc.

Home times

Child care workers must be vigilant to ensure that children are collected by adults who are known to them at home times. Parents should inform staff about who will be collecting the child if they cannot do so themselves. It is preferable for children to remain inside the building to await collection at home time. Every establishment should have a procedure for collecting children.

Emergency procedures

All establishments should have:

- Written emergency procedures
- Staff who have been trained in First Aid
- First Aid equipment
- An accident book for accurate recording of all incidents requiring First Aid
- Regular review of incidents to highlight areas of concern and follow-up action
- A planned programme of accident prevention

NOW ANSWER THESE QUESTIONS

1 How can accidents be prevented in child care establishments?
2 Why do you think children are most at risk at home?
3 What can the child care worker do to ensure children's safety during outdoor play?
4 How can children learn about road safety?
5 What safety precautions must be taken in places where children are cared for?

3 First Aid

Good supervision in a safe environment will ensure that accidents and injuries are kept to a minimum. However, it is vital for all child care workers to know how to deal with emergency situations and when to call for medical assistance.

FIRST AID FOR MINOR INJURIES

It is essential to remain calm when dealing with an injured child and reassure them that everything will be alright.

- **Burns/scalds.** Immerse in cold water for at least 10 minutes to reduce the temperature of the area.
- **Bleeding.** Minor bleeds must be cleaned and covered; major bleeds must be stopped by direct pressure as quickly as possible.
- **Nosebleeds.** Sit the child leaning forwards and pinch the soft part of the nose above the nostrils.
- **Sprains.** Treat with a combination of Rest, Ice, Compression and Elevation ('RICE)'.
- **Foreign body**. Children who have poked an

object into their nose or ears should be taken to the nearest Accident and Emergency Department where the object can be safely removed.

- **Choking.** Put the child over your knee, head down. Then:

  - Slap sharply between the shoulder blades up to five times.
  - Check to see if the object has become dislodged and is in the mouth.
  - Call for medical aid – take the child to the phone with you if you are alone.
  - Check 'ABC' (see **First Aid: The Recovery Position**, pages 8–9)
  - Try the back slaps again.

A FIRST AID BOX AND ITS CONTENTS

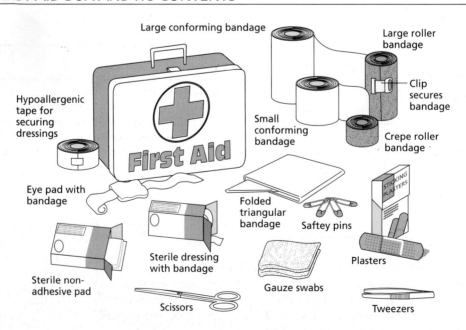

Large conforming bandage

Large roller bandage

Clip secures bandage

Hypoallergenic tape for securing dressings

Small conforming bandage

Crepe roller bandage

Eye pad with bandage

Folded triangular bandage

Saftey pins

STICKING PLASTERS

Plasters

Sterile dressing with bandage

Sterile non-adhesive pad

Gauze swabs

Scissors

Tweezers

ASTHMA

Asthma attacks are very frightening for children. During an attack the airways go into spasm, making breathing difficult, especially breathing out.

- Keep the child calm and reassure them.

- Encourage them to sit down and lean forwards against a support e.g. table.
- Help them to use their inhaler if available.
- If condition persists, call for an ambulance and contact parents.

DIABETES

This condition occurs when there is a disturbance in the way the body regulates the sugar concentrations in the blood, giving rise to hypoglycaemia (too little sugar in the blood) or hyperglycaemia (too much sugar in the blood). Both conditions eventually lead to unconsciousness but hyperglycaemia usually develops slowly. It is most likely that a diabetic child will experience episodes of low blood sugar (hypoglycaemia).

The treatment for hypoglycaemia is as follows:

- If the child is conscious, give sugar, e.g. glucose tablets, chocolate or a sugary drink.
- The condition should improve within a few minutes. If so, offer more sweetened food or drink.
- Inform parents, who should seek necessary advice to stabilise the condition.

AN UNCONSCIOUS CHILD

Assess the child's condition:

- Check for response – call the child's name/pinch the skin.
- Shout for help.
- Open the airway and check for breathing.
- Check the pulse.
- Act on your findings.

Recovery position
An unconscious child who is breathing and has a pulse should be put into recovery position to keep the airway clear by preventing choking on the tongue or vomit. Check for breathing and the pulse until medical help arrives (see **First Aid**, pages 8–9).

INFORMING PARENTS

Parents must be informed of all injuries which occur to their child, however minor, with as much detail as possible about how the injury happened. This ensures continuity of care between the establishment and home. If the child needs to talk about their experiences with their parents, they will then be prepared to deal with any consequences.

Accident book
Every accident should be recorded in an accident book, with details of time, date, who was involved and what happened, details of the injury and treatment and who was informed of the accident.

NOW ANSWER THESE QUESTIONS

1 What should the First Aid box in a child care establishment contain?
2 What is the policy in your setting for reporting and recording accidents?
3 Explain why it is important to remain calm in the event of an accident.
4 What is the emergency procedure for dealing with a child who is choking?
5 What is recorded in the accident book?

First Aid: The Recovery Position

The illustrations below show the steps to be followed when placing a child in the recovery position.

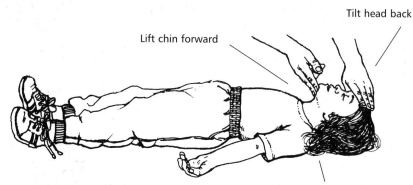

Tilt head back

Lift chin forward

Make sure airway is clear

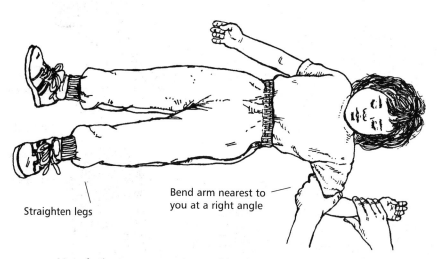

Straighten legs

Bend arm nearest to you at a right angle

Move furthest arm across chest and bend it

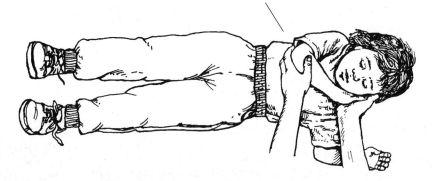

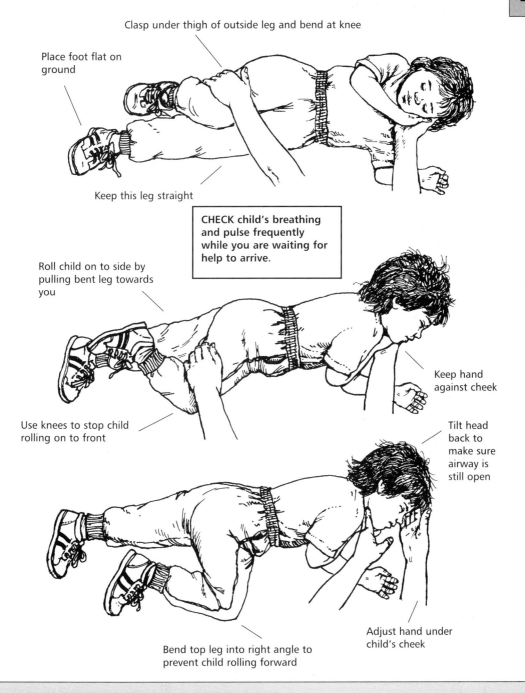

Clasp under thigh of outside leg and bend at knee

Place foot flat on ground

Keep this leg straight

CHECK child's breathing and pulse frequently while you are waiting for help to arrive.

Roll child on to side by pulling bent leg towards you

Keep hand against cheek

Use knees to stop child rolling on to front

Tilt head back to make sure airway is still open

Adjust hand under child's cheek

Bend top leg into right angle to prevent child rolling forward

NOW ANSWER THESE QUESTIONS

1   When would you place a child in the recovery position?
2   Why is the recovery position important in the care of a casualty?
3   What vital signs must be checked regularly whilst waiting for help to arrive?

Child Protection

Because child care workers are in close contact with young children every day, they are in a position to take an active role in protecting them. They may be a trusted adult whom a child chooses to confide in, or they may be alerted by changes in behaviour or physical signs of abuse. It is important to know what the signs of abuse are and what action should be taken.

Child carers who are with children for long periods are well placed to notice and record any changes in their behaviour

TYPES OF CHILD ABUSE

Physical abuse involves someone deliberately causing physical harm or hurt to a child. It includes the use of excessive force when feeding or changing a baby and unacceptable physical 'punishments'.

Sexual abuse is the involvement of children in sexual activities that they do not understand and cannot give their consent to.

Emotional abuse includes constant threats, shouting, taunting and verbal attacks. Not meeting childrens' needs in any area of development will also cause emotional damage.

Neglect involves persistently failing to meet the basic essential needs of children and failing to look after their health, safety and well-being.

SIGNS AND SYMPTOMS OF CHILD ABUSE

Always act in the best interests of the child and follow up any concerns you may have about physical injuries to a child or changes in their behaviour. Abuse affects the whole child and all areas of development. Physical and behavioural signs may apply to all types of abuse, e.g. a child who is being physically abused may also show changes in their behaviour.

Physical signs
- Failure to thrive
- Unusual bruising, finger or hand marks above the knee, on the body – not caused by everyday rough and tumble
- Burns
- Poor hygiene
- Bite marks
- Inappropriate clothing

Behavioural signs
- Clinging to or cowering from carer inappropriately

- Fear and apprehension, demonstrating a lack of trust in adults
- Unusually withdrawn
- Unusually aggressive
- Behaviour in role play (or small world or imaginative play) may indicate that the child is being abused.

Indicators of neglect
- Constant hunger, large appetite and poor growth – failure to thrive
- Inadequate clothing for the weather, dirty clothes, seldom washed
  Constant ill-health – nappy rash, stomach upsets, diarrhoea
- Poor personal hygiene, dull, matted hair, wrinkled skin, skin folds
- Constant tiredness and lack of energy
- Repeated accidental injuries
- Lateness at school
- Poor social relationships

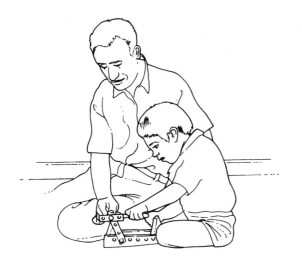

Spend time with the child and let them know you value them.

It may be possible then to discuss your concerns with parents, who may be able to provide a satisfactory explanation.

Supporting the child
Support the child who is the focus of your concern, giving them time and letting them know that you value them. It is important to provide activities which will help them to release their emotions – maybe anger and anxiety – and to give them the opportunity to talk about how they feel.

Observation
Skills in observation are essential to recognise and understand the effects of child abuse. Child carers who are with children for a large proportion of the time are well placed to notice any physical signs and/or changes in their behaviour.

Recording
Your observations, should be dated and signed. This will provide a reliable record of how the child is developing and should cover changes in behaviour and other areas of concern. Accurate records are important because they provide evidence of your concerns.

Reporting
Report any worrying signs and discuss anything that concerns you with a senior colleague, or with a health visitor if you work alone. They will advise you about the procedures for recording and reporting child protection issues.

Roles and responsibilities
In every establishment there should be a **designated person** who has specific responsibility for child protection and refers to and liaises with Social Services. All child care workers should know who that person is. They also need to know who they are directly responsible to, so that they can discuss concerns about the children, liaise, share information and plan effectively.

Working as a team
Team work includes working with professionals from other agencies including social workers, health visitors, police officers, NSPCC child protection officers and play therapists.

Referral
All professionals working with children have a duty to be vigilant and report any suspicions to the appropriate agency, usually Social Services.

NOW ANSWER THESE QUESTIONS
1   What are the different types of child abuse?
2   What are the signs of physical abuse?
3   Describe some behavioural signs of abuse.
4   What is the role of the child care worker in identifying and reporting signs of abuse?
5   Why is it important to involve parents/carers in early enquiries into suspected abuse?

6 Children's Outings

Child care workers must be able to plan an appropriate outing for children and to ensure their safety at all times. They must choose an outing that is consistent with the age/stage of development of the children, be aware of the statutory requirements, involve the parents/carers and be prepared for the unexpected.

BENEFITS OF OUTINGS

Outings with young children should be educational and fun

An outing is any trip away from the usual care and education setting. It can range from a visit to the shops to a whole day away. With thorough planning, it should be an enjoyable and educational experience for the children.

Outings give children an opportunity to:

- Benefit from new and unfamiliar experiences
- Learn about a specific area or the environment generally
- Follow up an interest or educational topic
- Meet new people

CHOOSING WHERE TO GO

The following factors are of paramount importance when considering taking children on an outing:

- Safety
- Appropriate clothing
- Food/refreshment
- Necessary equipment
- Involving parents

Deciding where to take the children can be relatively straightforward – there may be a local venue which has been visited successfully by other groups from your setting. However, when planning any trip, consider the following:

1 The **age** and **stage of development** of the children. There are differences in physical capabilities between average children from 1–7 years as well as variations in concentration levels and intellectual skills. Choose a destination which meets the needs of all the age groups you are taking.

2 **Learning outcomes.** Think about what you want the children to learn from the trip. Whether it is a trip to the library or a day at a farm, the aim of the outing is to benefit the children.

Adult help

A general guide for ratios on trips away from the setting is:

Children 0–2 years: 1 adult : 1 child
Children 2–5 years: 1 adult : 2 children
Children 5–8 years: 1 adult : 5 children

It is essential to have a higher adult/child ratio on any outing away from the establishment. There may be increased risks due to traffic, the unfamiliar surroundings (and lack of the usual physical boundaries) and the change from the normal routine. Remember also that you may need extra people to carry equipment, such as First Aid box, picnic/snacks and educational resources etc.

Travelling time

A remote destination can mean the difference between spending a morning, afternoon or whole day away.

It is vital to make sure that the journey will not be too tiring and that the time spent at the venue will be of value. Children do not like spending a disproportionate amount of time travelling.

Cost

If there is an entry fee or travelling costs, this may make the outing too expensive for some children in your establishment. Check whether there is enough funding to cater for all the children.

Transport

- Is the venue within walking distance?
- If not, can people offer lifts? Is there an establishment mini-bus?
- Do drivers have appropriate insurance?
- Do they have child restraints in their cars?

If arranging transport with an outside organisation, make sure that:

- They are insured
- The vehicle is large enough to seat everyone – adults and children
- There are sufficient child restraints, e.g. booster seats, seatbelts etc.
- The vehicles are safe

STAGES IN THE PLANNING PROCESS

1 Research into the destination, e.g. find out about opening times and accessibility for children. It may be possible to make an exploratory visit – if so, find out about toilet facilities/picnic areas/refreshments/First Aid provision/access for the disabled.
2 Decide on travel routes.
3 Prepare a timetable for the day. Everyone will need to know times of departure and arrival. Ensure that your programme is practical and there is enough time to do everything that you have planned for.
4 Make a list of equipment to take with you, e.g. First Aid kit, labels for the children, camera, money, audio tapes for the journey, worksheets and bags for collecting items of interest. Ask children to bring items with them, e.g. packed lunch, wet weather wear, pencils and paper etc.

5 Consult parents. It is necessary to get written consent from parents for any trip away from the establishment. They will need to know about the cost, the day's programme, transport, special requirements – lunch, clothing etc. A letter home with a consent slip is the best way to achieve this, perhaps combined with posters or notices displayed in the establishment.
6 Prepare the children for the trip. Show them leaflets and pictures and tell them stories to explain what will be happening during the outing. Stress the safety factors.

FOLLOW-UP WORK

Children should be encouraged to record their experience by completing a drawing or writing a story or poem. A display or interest table which incorporates the photographs taken on the trip is also beneficial.

NOW ANSWER THESE QUESTIONS

1 What are the benefits of taking children on outings?
2 Why do you need to provide a higher adult/child ratio on outings?
3 What are the stages in the planning process for an outing?
4 What contribution may parents make to outings?

Development 1– 4 Years

In order for child care workers to stimulate children's development, it is necessary to understand the factors that influence development and to know the developmental stages, so that appropriate activities can be provided to enable a child to progress to the next stage.

DEVELOPMENT BY STAGES

All children follow the same stages of development but the rate (speed) of development varies.

Whatever the age of the child, they must be able to sit unaided before they are ready to learn to walk. There is a wide variation in what is considered to be 'normal' development, e.g. one child may walk at 9 months and another may begin to walk at 18 months. Both fall within the 'normal' range.

When a skill is achieved, children need the opportunity to practise it so that they become competent before accomplishing the next stage.

ENCOURAGING PHYSICAL SKILLS

Gross motor

Children are more likely to become confident and physically well co-ordinated if they are offered a safe and stimulating environment in which to explore and experiment.

They should be offered the opportunity to:

- Learn and practise new skills, e.g. climbing stairs, walking, propelling a tricycle
- Learn from experience in a secure environment

- Play outdoors with supervision, e.g. in the park, at nursery
- Explore new and different environments, e.g. swimming, soft play areas

Fine motor

The activities shown below can all play a valuable part in stimulating children's hand/eye co-ordination:

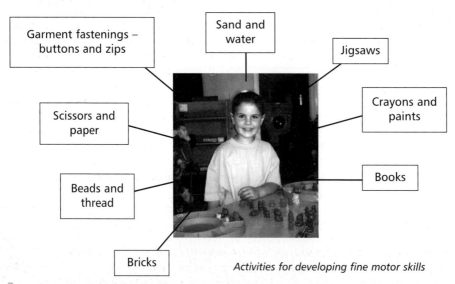

Garment fastenings – buttons and zips

Sand and water

Jigsaws

Scissors and paper

Crayons and paints

Beads and thread

Books

Bricks

Activities for developing fine motor skills

BENEFITS OF PHYSICAL EXERCISE

1 Improves digestion, stimulates the appetite and helps to prevent constipation
2 Helps the development of the lungs by encouraging full expansion
3 Improves the circulation as the heart muscle is strengthened, giving a healthy glow
4 Strengthens muscles and improves muscle tone
5 Improves co-ordination
6 Encourages achievement which boosts confidence and self-esteem
7 Gives a feeling of well-being
8 Promotes rest and sleep
9 Provides an outlet for surplus energy and aggression and an opportunity to make a noise and have a good time

Outdoor play should be safe and stimulating

PHYSICAL EXERCISE IN DAY CARE AND NURSERY ENVIRONMENTS

Children should have the opportunity to play outdoors every day, preferably with open access to a playground or grassed area supervised by qualified staff. A watchful adult is essential. This play provision should be available and accessible to all children with and without disabilities, boys and girls. It could include:

- A separate area for toddlers, where they can be safe from boisterous 3- and 4-year-olds
- Climbing frames and slides with safe surfaces beneath, to encourage climbing skills with the 'reward' of a slide at the end
- Assault/obstacle courses for the older children to improve confidence, co-ordination and self-esteem
- Hoops and balls to encourage development of throwing, catching and rolling skills
- Buckets of water and brushes to 'paint' the walls and paths
- Trolleys, tricycles and prams
- Water trough and a variety of toys

NOW ANSWER THESE QUESTIONS

1 Why is it important to provide a stimulating environment for physical development?
2 Why is physical exercise important for the well-being of the child?
3 What type of equipment/activities are suitable for outdoor play between 1–4 years?

Gross Motor Skills

The table below shows the stages of gross motor physical development from 1-7 years including the range of ages at which particular skills may be achieved, and the average age at which the skills are acquired.

SKILL	AGE-RANGE	STAGE OF DEVELOPMENT	AV. AGE OF ACHIEVEMT.
Walking	8–15 months	• Gets into the sitting position from lying, sits alone, pulls to stand and may stand alone. • Moves around by crawling, bottom-shuffling, bear walking or crawling. • Tries to climb upstairs, sometimes successfully.	12 months
	8–18 months	• Stands alone. • Walks alone, feet wide apart, arms raised for balance. • Falls easily especially on stopping; cannot yet avoid obstacles. • Sits down by falling back on bottom or forwards onto arms. • Stands without help from people or objects. • Kneels on the floor.	15 months
	12–24 months	• Walks confidently, arms down, stops without falling. • Carries large toys and pushes trollies etc. • Runs but falls often. • Squats to pick up objects from the floor. • Tries to kick a ball.	18 months
	18 months – 2½ years	• Runs safely, stopping and starting easily. • Can jump with two feet together. • Kicks a ball.	2 years
	2½–4 years	• Stands and walks on tiptoe. • Stands on one foot briefly. • Walks forwards, sideways and backwards. • Kicks a ball hard in the intended direction.	3 years
	3–5 years	• Stands, walks and runs on tiptoe. • Stands on one foot for a few seconds. • Hops on either foot. • Hops forwards for a few metres, keeping balance.	4 years

SKILL	AGE-RANGE	STAGE OF DEVELOPMENT	AV. AGE OF ACHIEVEMT.
Climbing	8–18 months	• May crawl upstairs forwards and downstairs backwards.	12 months
	12–18 months	• Climbs forwards into a small chair and turns to sit.	15 months
	15–21 months	• Walks upstairs with hand(s) held, comes down safely. • May walk down forwards with hands held, one step at a time. • Climbs forward into adult sized chair and turns to sit.	18 months
	18 months – 2½ years	• Walks up and downstairs alone, holding rail with two feet to a step. • Tries to climb small apparatus with varied success.	2 years
	2½ – 4 years	• Walks upstairs with one foot to each step, downstairs with two feet to a step. • Climbs ladder to nursery slide and attempts climbing frames .	3 years
	3–5 years	• Walks up and downstairs in adult manner. • Agile climber, increasing in confidence and daring	4 years
Propelling wheeled toy	9–18 months	• Pushes trolley or other wheeled toy.	15 months
	12 months – 2 years	• Steers wheeled trolley around obstacles, reversing etc.	18 months
	18 months – 2 ½ years	• Propels a small trike by pushing with the feet.	2 years
	2½ – 4 years	• Pedals tricycle, steering round obstacles.	3 years

NOW ANSWER THESE QUESTIONS

1 What are the stages/ages in the development of walking/running skills between 1–4 years?
2 How could you encourage a child to walk alone?
3 Describe the process of learning to ride a tricycle using the pedals and brakes.
4 Describe the stages of learning to climb stairs.

Physical Development 4–7 Years

Child care workers need to be aware of the importance of physical exercise and how to provide for it, so that they can plan appropriate and exciting activities to stimulate physical development in a safe and secure environment indoors and outdoors.

THE ROLE OF THE CHILD CARE WORKER

All child care workers must have a sound knowledge of child development so that:

- They can plan activities which will help the children to progress to the next stage of development
- Their expectations are realistic
- They can identify children who are not making progress

Providing for exercise

Providing for children's exercise is an important aspect of working with children of all ages and abilities. It is possible to choose physical activities which meet the individual needs of the children in your care. There may be some limitations in homes and establishments involving space and money for equipment. However, with thought and planning it is possible to create an effective environment for physical exercise.

The adult child care worker should be available to:

- Set goals for activities and explain rules
- Promote equal opportunities by being a positive role model and joining in with the play, encouraging ALL the children to participate in ALL activities and to be tolerant of one another
- Provide positive reinforcement and encouragement of children's achievements
- Act as a referee to show fairness, and prevent arguments developing
- Help and reassure the children when necessary
- Extend the activity and create new stimulation for the children

An example of an 'assault course' for young children

Equipment to balance on

Equipment to go over

Equipment to go under

Equipment to go through

EQUIPMENT

A wide range of equipment is available for promoting exercise for children. Exercise helps to increase energy, stamina, strength, suppleness, agility, co-ordination and balance, and children's confidence will grow as a result.

- Slides encourage climbing.
- Swings encourage co-ordination in movement and balance.
- Bicycles develop balance and co-ordination to turn pedals, steer, stop and start.
- Trampolines encourage jumping, hopping, somersaults, balance and co-ordination.
- Climbing frames encourage agility, strength, balance and suppleness.

- Climbing nets/rope ladders encourage balance, strength and co-ordination.
- Balls and beanbags help develop hand-eye co-ordination and catching/throwing skills.

All of this equipment can be modified to make it accessible to children with special needs. Some simple adaptations to the school playground such as painting footsteps, hopscotch games, numbered squares etc. onto the tarmac can increase the amount of exercise taken by children and stimulate play-time activity.

PLANNING A PLAY AREA

Ideally, a children's play area should be away from roads, open water and building sites, although this is not always possible if it is attached to a nursery or infant school. It should incorporate areas where the children can be quiet as well as areas where they can run around and let off steam. The children may help in planning the area, and equipment must be linked to the stage of development of the children but at the same time provide some challenges. An area for gardening and exploring the natural world encourages interest in how things grow and ecology.

Ideally, there should be space for games that all the children can play, e.g. football, rounders, netball, cricket.

INDOOR EXERCISE

Indoor exercise should not just be for rainy days. There are a lot of opportunities for exercise which are suitable for an indoor setting, for example:

- Dance and drama
- Gymnastics
- Team games
- Ring games
- PE with apparatus
- PE using mime and music

Music arouses emotional and physical responses. Young children tend to have few inhibitions and move naturally in time to music. Using musical instruments in the setting or tapes and CDs can encourage enjoyable exercise in children and stimulate their spatial awareness, balance, co-ordination and agility. This is a non-competitive activity which helps to build relationships and encourages sharing and consideration for others.

Children may also be members of groups or organisations that offer physical exercise as part of their activities, e.g. Rainbows, Beavers, Brownies, Cub Scouts etc.

NOW ANSWER THESE QUESTIONS

1 Describe the role of the child care worker in providing opportunities for exercise for children.
2 Why is it important for an adult to be available during periods of physical activity?
3 What types of equipment are suitable for promoting physical exercise?
4 What are the benefits of using music during physical exercise?

10 Fine Motor Development

Fine motor development involves the growing ability of the child to use the hands in co-ordination with the eyes. It ranges from the reflex grasping of the new-born infant to the delicate actions of older children threading needles.

The chart shows the progress expected of children between 1 year and 7 years 11 months and provides ideas for suitable activities to stimulate this area of development.

AGE	AVERAGE STAGE OF DEVELOPMENT	STIMULATING ACTIVITIES
12 months	Picks up small objects with pincer grasp. Watches toys fall after throwing them Points to desired objects Bangs cubes together Primitive tripod grasp	Encourage self-feeding with finger foods – with constant supervision Books with bright, bold pictures Bricks, posting boxes, shape-sorters Large-piece jigsaws, chunky crayons
15 months	Builds two-brick tower Holds a crayon with a palmar grasp Uses index finger to point to pictures in books Holds a spoon but turns it upside down before reaching the mouth	Construction bricks, e.g. Duplo, Sticklebricks Musical toys – xylophone, baby keyboard etc. Touch button books to play a tune, repeat a phrase etc. Tactile toys with different textures Offer spoon at feeding times
18 months	Delicate pincer grasp Tripod grasp of crayon/pencil Scribbles on paper with random dots Builds three-brick tower Enjoys picture books Usually feeds self efficiently with spoon	Sand play with raking, sieving, measuring toys Water play – pouring jugs, funnels Dough with rolling pins, cutters etc. Crayons and paper Finger paints
2 years	Picks up small items neatly and places down skilfully Unwraps small sweet efficiently Circular scribble, copies straight line Turns pages of a book singly Uses spoon skilfully	Small world play – Playmobil figures Tabletop toys, jigsaws Preparing fruit salads
2 years 6 months	Builds tower of seven or more bricks Recognises small details in pictures and photographs Copies straight line, circle, 'T' and 'V'	Small world play Peeling fruit, e.g. banana, satsuma Drawing and painting activities Looking at books
3 years	Builds tower of nine or ten bricks Builds a bridge with three bricks after demonstration or from a model, using two hands co-operatively Cuts with scissors Threads large beads onto a shoelace Holds pencil in preferred hand with good control and copies a cross and some letters e.g. 'V', 'H', 'T' Eats using spoon and fork Can undo and fasten buttons	Toys to dress and undress, small world playhouses or similar Preparing snacks – spreading sandwiches, peeling fruit Jigsaws Picture lotto Water play – pouring and measuring Collage – cutting and sticking Painting Drawing Dressing up clothes

AGE	AVERAGE STAGE OF DEVELOPMENT	STIMULATING ACTIVITIES
4 years	Builds tower of ten or more bricks Builds many bridges with three bricks Builds steps with six bricks after demon- stration Threads small beads onto a necklace Draws a person with head, body, arms and legs Draws a house on request Brushes teeth Skilful with spoon and fork	Bricks and blocks Threading with laces using beads of different shape, size and colour Cutting out shapes with scissors Dough and clay with cutters etc. Stencils for drawing around Cooking activities – measuring, spooning liquids, cracking eggs, making sandwiches, cutting up fruit and vegetables, decorating cakes and buns Carpenter's tools for hammering, screwing etc.
5 years	May thread needle and sew large stitches Builds four steps from ten bricks Grasps and adjusts pencil for comfort Writes some letters, may write name Draws house with door, windows, chimney etc. Counts fingers on one hand with index finger of the other hand Names the primary colours	As above and: Sewing activities Drawing, sticking – lots of creative activities Imaginative play, e.g. Post Office, hospital, hairdresser's, involving delicate movements Colouring activities Writing activities Tracing Knitting, weaving
6 years	Carefully aligns cubes when building May build intricate models with construction sets, e.g. Lego Holds a pen/cil with adult grasp and confines writing to a small area of the paper Catches a ball with one hand Ties shoelaces	As above and: Construction toys, bricks Small world play Junk modelling Ball games Board games using dice Wrapping parcels
7 years	May write with letters joined Sews with smaller, neater stitches May knit with simple stitches	Writing cards, letters etc. Sewing, embroidery, cross stitch, weaving Knitting using a pattern with a desired outcome

NOW ANSWER THESE QUESTIONS

1 What sort of activities would you provide for a 1–2-year-old child to encourage hand/eye co-ordination?
2 What fine motor skills is the average three-year-old capable of?
3 What is the sequence of hand/eye co-ordination between 4–7 years?
4 How can knowledge of this area of development help with planning activities for children in a nursery setting for 3–5-year-olds?

11 Physical Care – the Role of the Adult

Caring for children includes meeting their physical needs in a manner which recognises their individual differences and is consistent with the wishes of the child's family. Providing physical care promotes children's development by increasing their confidence, boosting self-esteem and giving them a sense of well-being.

HYGIENE ROUTINES

The role of the child care worker is to provide for children's personal hygiene, helping them to become independent by encouraging them to care for themselves. The wishes of the family must always be established so that consistency of care is maintained and there is no breach of cultural or religious practices.

Hair should be brushed and combed regularly if possible, especially after a nursery or school session. Combing helps to prevent the spread of headlice by breaking the legs of the louse.

Hair washing depends upon the wishes of the family. It is not necessary to wash children's hair every day unless it is full of food or paint! Rastafarian children may have dreadlocks, and may or may not wash their hair.

Skin. Regular washing of the hands is important especially before meals and after going to the toilet. Some families bath their children daily; others do not. It depends on the personal preferences of the family and the needs of the child. Children with skin conditions like eczema may need special products.

Regular child care routines may reveal signs of infection or illness in a child, e.g.:

- Rashes on the skin (may look like bruising on black skin)
- Sore/itchy areas
- Pale, flushed or clammy skin
- Headlice
- Abnormal marks or bruising

If you see any of the above signs, you should report them to a senior member of staff immediately.

Teeth. Toothbrushes can be introduced before teeth erupt. Young babies like to play with the brush and copy the brushing action of other children and adults. This early introduction can help to prevent problems and resistance to cleaning the teeth when the time comes. Children should be encouraged to brush their teeth morning and night and between meals if possible. Fluoride toothpastes offer the most protection to the teeth, but eating healthy foods and trying not to eat between meals also improves dental health.

Bathing together can be fun!

EQUIPMENT

The type and amount of equipment required to provide physical care for children at home is a matter of personal/parental preference. In day care children do need their own:

- Sponge or flannel
- Towel
- Toothbrush
- Brush/comb

CLOTHING AND FOOTWEAR

Clothing for children must be:

- Comfortable and loose enough to allow for movement
- Easily washed
- Appropriate for the season – extra layers of thin garments are warmer than one thick jumper

Footwear should:

- Protect the feet without rubbing or chafing the skin
- Allow room for growth and fit well around the heel
- Be flexible and allow free movement
- Have an adjustable fastener

Vigorous physical play requires flexible, comfortable clothing

REST AND SLEEP

Children need rest and adequate sleep to help them to develop to their full potential. Each child is unique and will require different amounts of rest and sleep depending on their individual needs. When children are tired they need to be able to rest in a quiet area and do some restful activities if they do not want to sleep.

Helping children to prepare for a daytime nap will encourage them to sleep. Some may need a comforter, some soothing music or a story. Some may like their head stroked or hand held. It is important for the child care worker to know the individual preferences of all children in their care. Dimming the light and keeping noise to a minimum will aid sleep during the day or at night.

At night a regular routine will encourage babies and children to settle down to sleep, e.g. teatime, followed by bathtime, followed by bedtime story.

In a day care establishment extra care is required to prevent the spread of infection at sleep times. Children must be settled in clean bedding in a well ventilated room, and the temperature should be reduced if children are sleeping under duvets or blankets.

NOW ANSWER THESE QUESTIONS

1 Which signs of infection or illness may be observed when attending to children's physical care?
2 How can the child care worker encourage good dental health?
3 What factors should be taken into account when selecting clothing for children?
4 What factors influence the rest/sleep needs of young children?
5 How can children be encouraged to rest and sleep?

12 Encouraging Independence

Children usually want to do things for themselves, and it is the role of the child care worker to encourage this independence within safe limits. Children do not acquire skills straight away – they need time to practise and a positive environment where each achievement is recognised and praised, however small it may seem.

TOILET-TRAINING

Children can only be toilet-trained successfully when their nervous system is mature enough to recognise the sensation of a full bowel or bladder. The table below shows the sequence of this area of development. Remember that some children with special needs may be incontinent. They should have the opportunity to become independent if possible, but will need privacy and special sensitivity on the part of the child care worker.

For successful training children must be:

- Physically ready to be trained
- Able to communicate their need for the potty or toilet
- Keen and willing to learn
- Shown what to do by watching other children and adults
- Helped by an encouraging adult
- Treated with patience and understanding

STAGE	AGE	DEVELOPMENT	ROLE OF CARER
1	Birth – 12 months	• Reflex emptying of bowel and bladder • May indicate discomfort resulting from a dirty or wet nappy	• Regular nappy changing with stimulation – talking and physical contact making this a pleasurable experience for the child
2	12–18 months	• Growing awareness of when they have urinated or passed a stool • May begin to connect the sensation of passing urine or faeces with the end result	• Regular changing • Potty becomes a familiar object but no pressure to use it • Positive role models • Lots of conversation during changing and when others use the potty or toilet
3	18–24 months	• Begin to know when they are about to pass urine or faeces but not yet able to give a reliable warning • May tell you when they have 'been'	• Potty available if child wants to sit on it • Offer potty with signs of a bowel movement, but no pressure to use it • Periods with no nappy allows child to connect the process with the end result • Lots of praise and smiles if child uses potty

STAGE	AGE	DEVELOPMENT	ROLE OF CARER
4	From 2 years	• Able to give sufficient warning that they need the potty or toilet • Growing ability to control bowel and bladder muscles until it is convenient • Accidents will inevitably happen!	• Easy-to-remove clothing • Taking potty to different rooms and on outings (plus a change of clothes!) • Begin to use the toilet with training seat • A step will help the child get on and off without help • Sympathetic and under-standing approach – the child will probably be very upset when accidents occur

SOCIAL SKILLS

Eating

Once children have developed the necessary physical skills they will gradually begin to feed themselves in a manner which is socially acceptable to their own culture if they are given the opportunity to practise. Babies normally finger-feed from 6 months onwards, gradually using implements – e.g. a spoon and cup – from about 12 months onwards. Some children may continue to use their fingers before progressing to a spoon and fork and then, from 3–4 years, a knife and fork.

For children to become self-reliant feeders they need:

- Opportunity to practise and make the inevitable mess
- Praise and encouragement for their efforts
- Opportunity to control their own eating, choosing from what is available
- Food that is easy to eat – i.e. that is cut into small pieces, or food that they can cut up easily themselves
- Sociable mealtimes. Families eating together around a table, or groups of children with an adult, make mealtimes more fun

- Comfortable seating so that they can easily reach their food – e.g. a high chair for a toddler, or an appropriate chair for a child
- Positive role models

Dressing

Children will gradually be able to dress themselves as their physical development progresses. Allowing them to choose which clothes to wear, giving them time in an unhurried atmosphere and buying garments with easy fasteners will encourage this.

They will find it easier to take off and put on shoes if the fasteners are easy to manage – Velcro and buckles are easier than laces. Children may not be able to tie shoelaces until they are 6–7 years of age.

Washing

Having a step by the washbasin at home, or child-height sinks in child care establishments enable children to achieve independence. Care should be taken that the hot water does not reach high temperatures and supervision is required to prevent overflowing sinks.

NOW ANSWER THESE QUESTIONS

1 How does the carer know when the child is ready for toilet training?
2 How can the adult encourage a child to become toilet-trained?
3 How can children be encouraged to become independent feeders?
4 How can the child carer enable children to dress themselves?

A Healthy Diet

Good nutrition is essential for health. Eating habits are established at an early age. Child care workers need to ensure that children establish healthy eating patterns which will promote normal growth and development. You will need to know basic facts about food, the nutrients it contains and how to provide a diet which is acceptable and healthy for the children in your care.

ESSENTIAL NUTRIENTS

Essential nutrients found in food and drink are:

- Proteins
- Fats
- Carbohydrates
- Vitamins
- Minerals
- Fibre
- Water

Protein, fat, carbohydrate and water are present in the foods we eat in large quantities. Vitamins and minerals are only present in small quantities.

Proteins provide material for:

- Growth of the body
- Repair of the body

Types of proteins:

- **Animal**, first class or complete proteins, supply all ten of the essential amino acids.
- **Vegetable**, second class or incomplete proteins, supply some of the ten essential amino acids.

FOODS CONTAINING PROTEINS

Protein foods are made up of amino acids. There are ten essential amino acids.

Examples of protein foods include:

- Animal proteins: meat, fish, chicken, eggs, dairy foods
- Vegetable proteins: nuts, seeds, pulses, cereals

Carbohydrates provide:

- Energy
- Warmth

Types of carbohydrates:

- Sugars
- Starches

Carbohydrates are broken down into glucose before the body can use them. **Sugars** are quickly converted and are a quick source of energy. **Starches** take longer to convert so they provide a longer-lasting supply of energy.

Examples of carbo-hydrate foods include:

- Sugars: fruit, honey, sweets, beet sugar, cane sugar
- Starches: potatoes, cereals, beans, pasta

FOODS CONTAINING CARBOHYDRATES

Fats:

- Provide energy and warmth
- Store fat-soluble vitamins
- Make food pleasant to eat

Types of fats:

- Saturated
- Unsaturated
- Polyunsaturates

Saturated fats are solid at room temperature and come mainly from animal fats. **Unsaturated and polyunsaturated fats** are liquid at room temperature and come mainly from vegetable and fish oils.

Examples of foods containing fat include:

- Saturated: butter, cheese, meat, palm oil
- Unsaturated: olive oil, peanut oil
- Polyunsaturated: oily fish, corn oil, sunflower oil.

FOODS CONTAINING FATS

NOW ANSWER THESE QUESTIONS

1. Give two examples of complete proteins.
2. Give two examples of incomplete proteins.
3. What are the two types of carbohydrate?
4. What are the three types of fat?

5. What are the functions of:
   a) Proteins?
   b) Carbohydrates?
   c) Fats?

14 Vitamins and Minerals

Vitamins and minerals are only present in small quantities in the foods we eat. They are essential for growth, development and normal functioning of the body. A knowledge of which vitamins and minerals are present in the various foods we eat will enable the child care worker to ensure a well balanced diet which includes a variety of foods containing the essential vitamins and minerals.

VITAMINS

There are many nutrients which the body is able to store, and fat-soluble vitamins are an example of these. Water-soluble vitamins which cannot be stored must be eaten every day.

Different combinations of vitamins and minerals are found in different foods, so a varied selection of foods will ensure adequate supplies.

VITAMIN	FOOD SOURCE	FUNCTION	NOTES
A	• Butter, cheese, eggs, carrots, tomatoes	• Promotes healthy skin and good vision.	• Fat-soluble, can be stored in the liver. Deficiency causes skin infections, problems with vision. Avoid excess intake during pregnancy.
B	• Fish, meat, liver, green vegetables, beans, eggs	• Healthy working of muscles and nerves. Active in haemo-globin formation.	• Water-soluble, not stored in the body so a regular supply is needed. Deficiency results in muscle wasting, anaemia.
C	• Fruits and fruit juices (especially orange and blackcurrant), green vegetables	• Promotes healthy skin and tissue. Aids healing processes.	• Water-soluble, daily supply needed. Deficiency means less resistance to infection; extreme deficiency results in scurvy.
D	• Oily fish, cod liver oil, egg yolk; added to margarines and to milk	• Aids growth and maintenance of strong bones and teeth.	• Fat-soluble, can be stored by the body. Can be produced by the body by the action of sunlight on skin. Deficiency results in bones failing to harden and dental decay.
E	• Vegetable oils, cereals, egg yolk, nuts and seeds	• Promotes healing, aids blood clotting and fat metabolism.	• Fat-soluble, can be stored by the body.
K	• Green vegetables, liver, whole grains	• Needed for normal blood clotting, aids healing.	• Fat-soluble, can be stored by the body. Deficiency may result in delayed clotting, excessive bleeding.

MINERALS

Minerals are essential for good health. They are found in small quantities in food and can be stored in the body.

Healthy children eating a well balanced diet are unlikely to suffer from mineral deficiencies.

MINERAL	FOOD SOURCE	FUNCTION	NOTES
Calcium	• Cheese, eggs, fish, pulses	• Essential for growth of bones and teeth.	• Works with Vitamin D. Deficiency means that bones fail to harden (rickets) and leads to dental decay.
Fluoride	• Occurs naturally in water or may be added to water, toothpaste, drops and tablets.	• Makes tooth enamel more resistant to decay.	• There are arguments for and against adding fluoride to the water supply.
Iodine	• Water, seafoods, vegetables, added to salt	• Needed for proper working of the thyroid gland.	• Deficiency results in disturbance in the function of the thyroid gland.
Iron	• Meat, green vegetables, eggs, liver, dried fruit, esp. apricots, prunes, raisins	• Needed for the formation of haemo-globin in red blood cells.	• Vitamin C helps the absorption of iron. Deficiency results in anaemia causing lack of energy.
Phosphorus	• Fish, meat, eggs, fruit and vegetables	• Formation of bones and teeth, helps absorption of carbo-hydrate	• High intake is harmful to babies.
Potassium	• Meat, milk, cereals, fruit and vegetables	• Helps to maintain fluid balance.	• Deficiency is rare as potassium is found in a wide range of foods.
Sodium chloride	• Table salt, fish, meat, bread, processed foods	• Needed for fluid balance, formation of cell fluids blood, sweat, tears.	• Salt should not be added to food prepared for babies and young children.

NOW ANSWER THESE QUESTIONS

1 What is the advantage of a vitamin being fat-soluble?
2 Which vitamin helps the absorption of iron?
3 What is the function of:
   a) Vitamin C   b) Vitamin D   c) Iron   d) Calcium
4 Which vitamins need to be included in the diet every day? Why?
5 When might a child's intake of vitamins and minerals become restricted?

15 Food and Diet

Child care workers need to know how to make sure children have a well balanced diet. To do this they may have to take a number of factors into account. These may include different dietary principles or a child's medical condition. It is also important to be aware of the learning opportunities for children when they help to prepare food.

A BALANCED DIET

Food preparation activities can help children learn basic maths skills (see opposite)

A well balanced diet means that the intake of food provides all the nutrients that the body needs in the right quantities. This is achieved by eating a wide variety of foods every day, which means that there should be no deficiency of a particular nutrient. A varied diet gives children the opportunity to choose foods that they like and to taste and try new foods.

Variation in diets

Different diets have developed because of a number of factors including:

- Available foods
- Agricultural patterns
- Climate
- Geography
- Culture
- Class
- Lifestyle
- Religion

Each diet contains different foods but will provide a balance of essential nutrients. It is important for child care workers to talk to parents about food requirements to ensure that children's needs are met.

It is not possible to make general statements about the diets of different groups, only to suggest factors which may be important.

GROUP	DIETARY PRINCIPLES
Hindus	Many devout Hindus are vegetarian. Hindus eat no beef and drink no alcohol.
Muslims	May not eat pork or pork products. Alcohol is not permitted.
Jews	May not eat pork or shellfish. All other meat must be Kosher. Milk and meat are not used together in cooking.
Rastafarians	Mainly vegetarian. Whole foods are preferred. No products of the vine are eaten.
Christians	May avoid eating meat at certain times. Some foods may be given up in Lent.
Vegetarians	Do not eat meat and may restrict their intake of other animal products.
Vegans	Do not eat any animal products.

SPECIAL DIETS

Some children need a special diet for medical reasons. Examples are given in the table below.

CONDITION	DIET
Coeliac disease	Restrict intake of gluten which is found in wheat, barley, rye and oats.
Cystic fibrosis	Provide a high-protein, high-calorie diet. Vitamin and enzyme supplements are given.
Diabetes mellitus	Diet needs to be carefully controlled. Intake, especially of carbohydrate, must match the insulin given.
Obesity	Plan and promote healthy eating habits and daily exercise. Aim to prevent further weight gain and encourage a gradual weight loss.
Tooth decay	Discourage sweet foods. Promote a well balanced diet with whole foods which encourage chewing.

THE SOCIAL AND EDUCATIONAL ROLE OF FOOD

Children like to take part in cooking and food preparation at home and in nurseries and schools. These activities can create learning opportunities and enhance developmental skills.

Physical development
Gross motor skills are developed through mixing and beating. Manipulative skills are improved by cutting and stirring. Eye-hand co-ordination is improved by pouring, spooning out and weighing ingredients.

Intellectual development
Science concepts are learnt by seeing the effects of heat and cold on food. Maths skills are developed by counting, sorting and grading utensils, laying the table with sets of utensils for the correct number of people and weighing and measuring the ingredients.

Children can be encouraged to plan and make decisions about what and when they will eat.

Language development
Conversation and discussion can be encouraged at mealtimes. Adult interaction will promote and extend vocabulary.

Emotional development
Eating food is often a comfort and sharing food with others provides pleasure. Helping to prepare a meal will give children a sense of achievement.

Social development
Children can learn the skills of feeding independently. They can share with others and learn about appropriate behaviour at mealtimes.

NOW ANSWER THESE QUESTIONS

1   How is a well balanced diet achieved?
2   What restrictions do Vegans have on their diet?
3   Which food group in the diet needs to be controlled if a child has diabetes?
4   How can mealtimes help to promote language development?
5   What mathematical skills are used when laying a table for a meal?

16 Food Facts

Food is central to children's lives and it is important that food is prepared, stored and served safely and hygienically. What children eat may also be affected by poverty. A small number of children may have unexpected reactions to some foods.

FOOD AND POVERTY

Knowing about food and essential nutrients is very important. When money is tight, help needs to be concentrated on achieving an adequate diet within the budget and ability of the family. Knowing which cheaper foods contain essential nutrients will enable sensible advice to be offered.

Issues which influence children's diet in poorer families may include these factors:

- Money spent on food is less than the national average.
- Cooking facilities may be limited, e.g. in bed and breakfast accommodation.
- Shopping has to be local to avoid bus fares or carrying shopping long distances.
- Prices may be higher in rural or isolated areas.

FOOD ADDITIVES

Substances are often added to prepared foods to add colour, give flavour or preserve the food. Permitted food additives are given an 'E' number and are listed on the food label. For some children, erratic behaviour may be associated with particular additives in food.

To reduce additives in a child's diet:

- Use fresh foods as often as possible.
- Avoid processed foods.
- Read the food ingredient labels.

FOOD INTOLERANCE/ALLERGY

This may be caused by a number of factors including allergic response or an enzyme deficiency such as Coeliac disease or PKU (see **Food and Diet**, page 30). In rare cases children may be allergic to particular foods. Treatment for food intolerance must be carried out with medical supervision.

FOOD REFUSAL

Refusing to eat food provided and making a fuss about food at mealtimes is quite common among young children.

If the child is of normal body weight, thriving, and no medical condition is found by a doctor, then carers should be reassured. It is important that mealtimes should not become a battleground so child care workers should:

- offer food at mealtimes only
- avoid snacks between meals
- allow the child to eat according to appetite

- encourage participation in family and group mealtimes
- allow the child to eat independently
- not fuss about any mess when a child is learning to feed
- remove any remaining food without fuss
- promote mealtimes as a pleasant experience

FOOD SAFETY

For safety reasons, it is important to store food carefully. Always:

- Check 'use-by' and 'best before' dates
- Take chilled and frozen food straight home
- Use an insulated bag to transport chilled and frozen food
- Put chilled or frozen foods into the fridge or freezer as soon as possible

- Make sure the fridge temperature is between 0ºc and 5ºc
- Make sure the freezer temperature is below –18ºc
- Keep raw meat and fish in separate containers
- Store raw meat and fish at the bottom of the fridge

PREPARING FOOD

Food must be handled and prepared hygienically to avoid contamination. Always :

- Wash hands well before preparing food
- Cover any cuts with a waterproof dressing
- Wear an apron
- Tie hair back
- Avoid touching your nose and mouth or coughing and sneezing
- Disinfect work surfaces regularly and before preparing food
- Disinfect kitchen cloths daily and replace frequently
- Teach children how to prepare food safely

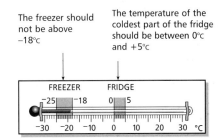

The freezer should not be above –18ºc

The temperature of the coldest part of the fridge should be between 0ºc and +5ºc

Safe temperatures for storing food in the fridge or freezer

COOKING FOOD

To keep food safe it is very important to cook it properly. Always:

- Defrost frozen food thoroughly before cooking
- Cook foods like chicken meat and fish thoroughly
- keep raw food and cooked food separately
- Cool cooked food quickly before storing in the fridge

- Cover food standing in the kitchen
- Only reheat cooked food once.
- Reheat cooked food until it is **very hot** all the way through.
- Cook eggs until the white and yolk are solid.
- Handle food with clean hands

NOW ANSWER THESE QUESTIONS

1 What do you need to know to help a family on a limited budget plan an adequate diet?
2 How can you reduce additives in a child's diet?
3 What temperature should the coldest part of the fridge be?
4 Where should you store raw meat?
5 What are the functions of artificial food additives?

Recognising Childhood Illnesses

It is very important to know about diseases that are common in childhood, and to be able to recognise the signs that indicate that a child is ill. You need to know what causes diseases and how diseases are spread. There are some signs of illness which are frequently seen and can be applied to most of the common illnesses children get.

CAUSES OF DISEASE

Diseases are caused by **pathogens**. The common name for pathogens is **germs.**

The most important pathogens are:

● Bacteria
● Viruses
● Fungi

Once pathogens are inside the body they multiply very rapidly. This period of time is called the **incubation period** and can last for a few days or weeks depending on the type of pathogen and disease.

Although the child is infected and infectious during the incubation period, they only begin to feel ill and have signs of the infection at the end of the incubation period.

THE GENERAL SIGNS OF CHILDHOOD ILLNESS

Note: These signs are always more worrying and significant in a baby or young child.

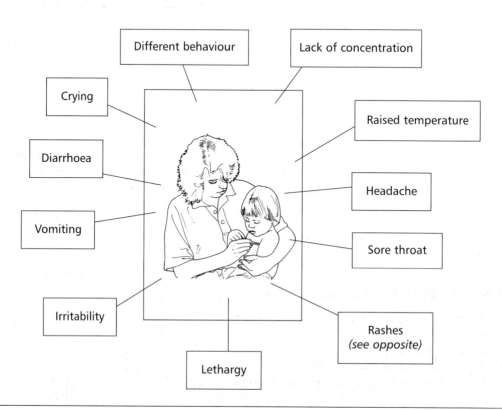

Different behaviour

Lack of concentration

Crying

Raised temperature

Diarrhoea

Headache

Vomiting

Sore throat

Irritability

Rashes
(see opposite)

Lethargy

METHODS OF SPREAD	EXAMPLE OF DISEASE
Droplet infection	Colds, coughs, measles, chickenpox, diphtheria
Touching infected people or material	Impetigo, athlete's foot, thrush
Drinking infected tap water	Gastro enteritis, polio, dysentery
Eating infected food	Food poisoning, gastro enteritis, diarrhoea, typhoid
Pathogens entering the body through a cut or graze	Tetanus, hepatitis, HIV

COMPARING RASHES OF INFECTIOUS DISEASES

One of the more common signs of a childhood infectious illness is a rash on the skin. These rashes have different features:

Chickenpox
The rash has well defined red spots which come in successive crops. The spots are red at first but develop into fluid-filled blisters. These dry off and form scabs which eventually drop off. Because spots keep on coming, the rash can take two or three weeks to disappear.

Measles
This is a red, blotchy, flat rash which starts at the top of the body and works donwards. You may see spots in the mouth (Koplik's spots). The rash usually takes 10–14 days to disappear.

Rubella
The spots are usually well defined and only last for a short time, usually 24 hours.

INFESTATIONS

Parasites obtain their food from humans and may affect children. Common parasites include:

- **Fleas:** small insects which feed on human blood. They live in clothing next to the skin.
- **Headlice:** insects which live on human hair, near to the scalp where they can easily bite the skin and feed on blood.
- **Ringworm:** a fungus seen as a raised red circle on the skin with a white scaly centre.
- **Threadworms:** small thread-like worms which live in the bowel.
- **Scabies:** tiny mites that burrow under the skin, causing itching and raised red spots.

NOW ANSWER THESE QUESTIONS

1 Give three examples of how diseases are spread.
2 Describe a measles rash.
3 List five general signs of illness.
4 Why do parasites live on humans?
5 Name two common parasites that infest children.

18

Childhood Illnesses

This chart lists the childhood illnesses you need to know about. It outlines the specific signs of the illness and the specific aspects of care required. Most illnesses will begin with the same general signs that a child is unwell (see **Recognising Childhood Illnesses**, page 34). The child will need all the general care outlined on pages 40–1 in addition to the specific care described here.

DISEASE	INCUBATION	SYMPTOMS	CARE
Chickenpox	14–16 days	Spots on chest and back. Red at first, becoming blisters, then forming a dry scab. Spots come in successive crops and are very itchy.	Discourage scratching and ease the itching by keeping the child cool and applying lotion such as calamine.
Coughs and colds	2–10 days	General signs of illness, nasal congestion, cough	General care, but monitor coughs carefully in case the chest becomes infected. Watch carefully in case other symptoms develop which would indicate a more serious illness. Consult doctor if unsure, especially with a baby.
Diarrhoea (caused by infected food or water)	2–7 days	Loose, frequent, watery stools, pains in the stomach	Give plenty of fluid to avoid dehydration. Consult a doctor for a baby or if the diarrhoea persists or the child shows signs of dehydration or other illness.
Diphtheria	2–6 days	Difficulty in breathing. White membrane forms in the throat.	Medical aid, usually, hospital treatment is needed.
Ear infections (otitis media)	Variable	Pain, discharge from the ear, high temperature	Medical aid, antibiotics and pain relief may be prescribed by a doctor.
Gastro enteritis (caused by infected food or dirty water)	1–14 days	Vomiting and diarrhoea	Medical aid. Hospital care may be needed. Give plenty of fluids. Oral rehydration solutions may be given.
Measles	7–14 days	Raised temperature, sore eyes, Koplik's spots, red blotchy rash which quickly spreads over the whole body	Medical aid. Eyes and ears may need special attention as complications include sensitivity to light and ear infections.

DISEASE	INCUBATION	SYMPTOMS	CARE
Meningitis	2–10 days	Symptoms include high temperature, headache, irritability, vomiting, rash, pain and stiffness in the neck, sensitivity to light.	Get medical aid. Early hospital treatment will be needed. It is very important to recognise meningitis early as the progress of this illness is very rapid and serious.
Mumps	14–21 days	Pain, tenderness and swelling around the jaw and ear, usually on one side of the face, then the other.	Doctor may advise pain relief. A rare complication in boys is inflammation of the testes.
Poliomyelitis (water-borne infection)	5–21 days	Headache, stiffness in neck and back, loss of movement and paralysis	Hospital care
Rubella	14–21 days	Mild general symptoms, rash lasting for about 24 hours	General care. Keep the child away from any women who may be pregnant as the rubella virus can damage the foetus.
Scarlet fever	2–6 days	Red tongue, sore throat, rash on face and body	Medical aid. Doctor may prescribe antibiotics.
Tetanus	4–21 days	Painful muscle spasms in neck and jaw	Hospital treatment required. Keep immunisation up to date.
Thrush (fungus infection)	Variable	White patches in the mouth, usually on the tongue and inside the cheeks. A baby may have a sore bottom.	Consult the doctor who will prescribe a specific treatment. Check that all feeding equipment is sterilised.
Tuberculosis	28–42 days	Cough, weight loss, investigation shows lung damage.	Medical aid. Specific antibiotics are given.
Whooping cough	7–14 days	Long bouts of coughing and choking, difficulty in breathing during the coughing, whooping noise as the child draws in breath. Vomiting during coughing bouts	Medical aid. Support during coughing bouts, reassurance. Give food after coughing if vomiting is a problem. Possible complicatons are permanent lung damage, brain damage, ear infections and bronchitis.

NOW ANSWER THESE QUESTIONS

1 Describe the stages of a chickenpox rash.
2 Why is it important to recognise meningitis early?
3 Describe two complications of whooping cough.

19 Childhood Conditions

There are some conditions and chronic illnesses which affect children and may be commonly encountered by child care workers. You will need to know about these so that you are able to meet the needs of the children and their parents.

ASTHMA

Asthma is a condition in which the airways in the lungs become narrowed. Allergy to substances such as pollen, dust, pet hair, causes the airways to swell. Spasms of the airways may cause further narrowing, making breathing difficult. The child wheezes and becomes breathless. Attacks vary in severity, but a bad attack can be very frightening. Severe asthma attacks are serious and require prompt medical aid.

Inhalers help to get medication into the lungs and relieve the affected airways. These medicines are called **bronchodilators** and help to reduce swelling and spasm in the airways at the time of an attack. Other medicines given by regular use of inhalers help to prevent attacks occurring.

There are different types of inhaler which children can learn to use. It is very important that a child's inhaler is immediately available

In an emergency
If a child in your care has an asthma attack:

- Keep calm
- Reassure the child
- Help them to use their inhaler
- Get medical aid if the attack does not begin to subside quickly

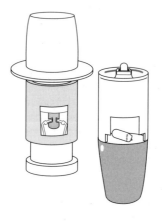

Different types of inhaler used by asthma sufferers

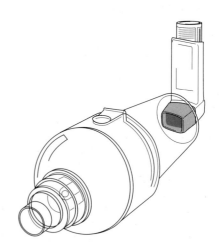

COELIAC DISEASE

A child with Coeliac disease is sensitive to gluten, a protein found in wheat, rye, barley, and oats. The lining of the small intestine becomes damaged and the child is unable to absorb food properly. The child does not grow normally, failing to gain weight satisfactorily, especially after weaning foods containing gluten have been introduced.

Children with the Coeliac condition must follow a diet which excludes gluten. This means that child care workers must be able to select the correct foods, usually fresh vegetables, fish, meat and dairy products. A knowledge of which foods contain gluten is essential. Detailed lists of suitable foods are available from the Coeliac Society.

CYSTIC FIBROSIS (CF)

An inherited condition, cystic fibrosis affects the lungs and digestive system. A child with cystic fibrosis produces very thick, sticky mucus which blocks the airways in the lungs, causing infection and breathing problems. Mucus also affects the flow of enzymes into the digestive tract, interfering with the absorption of food. Children with CF have repeated chest and breathing problems and poor growth rates.

Treatment for CF is intensive and will include:

- **Physiotherapy** to keep the lungs clear
- **Enzymes** given as tablets to aid digestion
- **Antibiotics** to help keep the lungs free from infection

The child care worker may be involved in the treatment of a child with CF.

DIABETES

This condition occurs when the pancreas produces insufficient amounts of insulin. Insulin controls the amount of sugar in the body. Too little will result in high levels of sugar accumulating in the blood and urine. This is dangerous and life-threatening.

Diabetes in children is treated with injections of insulin and a carefully controlled diet restricting carbohydrate intake. Children learn how to test their own blood and urine and to keep records of the results. They also learn about what they may eat. Often children administer their own injections of insulin.

Children with diabetes need to have their meals on time. They may need to eat snacks or a glucose drink before exercise or if they stay late at school or begin to feel unwell. Any cuts or grazes need careful attention because of the higher risk of infection.

Further information on diabetes can be found on page 7.

SICKLE CELL ANAEMIA

This is an inherited condition of haemoglobin formation, in which the red cells in the blood take on a characteristic sickle shape.

When the cells become sickle-shaped they tend to clump together, causing problems with circulation and precipitating a **painful crisis** during which children experience pain and swelling and feel very ill. Carers need to maintain a good diet and provide plenty of fluids, warmth and rest. Sometimes blood transfusions and other treatments are needed. Children will need reassurance and support during a crisis and co-operation with parents and the hospital will help the child to manage the condition.

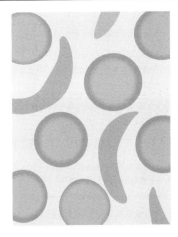

Normal and sickle red blood cells

NOW ANSWER THESE QUESTIONS

1 What are bronchodilators?
2 Which foods contain gluten?
3 What are the three main areas of treatment for cystis fibrosis?
4 Which substance controls the amount of sugar circulating in the body?
5 What is a 'painful crisis'?

Caring for Sick Children

As a child care worker you will need to know about the general care of a child who is unwell, both at home and in the child care and education setting. It is important to know when to pass on information to parents/carers and other professionals. There are important points that you should be aware of about giving medicines to children and how to store and manage them safely.

CARING FOR SICK CHILDREN AT HOME

Sick babies and children need to be with their main carer if possible. Changing the child's clothes and bedclothes frequently will help the child to feel more comfortable, as will combing their hair and washing their hands and face. Give an all-over wash if a bath is not possible. Keep the room warm (about 21°C) and well ventilated.

Children who are ill often need help with tasks that they can usually manage, e.g. washing or toileting. This is not unusual and is sometimes referred to as **regression**. They return to their previous independence when they are better.

Keep the child's environment:

● Well ventilated
● At a constant 21°C
● Shielded from direct light if the child is sensitive to this

Keeping up the intake of fluids, especially water, is very important and you should encourage the sick child to drink little and often. Babies and young children can easily become dehydrated, especially if they have diarrhoea. Dehydration is dangerous and you need to watch for signs of this.

Symptoms of dehydration include:

● A dry mouth
● Dry, loose skin
● Sunken eyes
● With babies, a sunken fontanelle

Food may be refused when a child is ill. This may not be serious at first as long as plenty of fluids are taken. Later you should tempt the child with small portions of colourful, attractive, easily managed and digested foods.

To keep the child occupied, choose activities which are not too difficult or demanding. Children often like to return to activities they enjoyed when they were younger and you should be prepared to adapt the normal routine to allow this.

MANAGEMENT OF A FEVER

A fever can flare up quickly in babies and young children, and a raised temperature shows that the body is under attack. A feverish child needs to be able to get rid of excess heat, so it is important to keep the room airy and cool. Removing a layer of clothing will help the cooling process. Constantly observe the child and supervise them closely. If possible give frequent drinks of water. A normal temperature is 37°C.

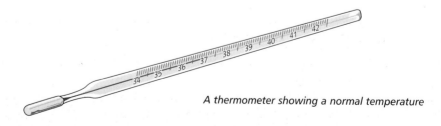

A thermometer showing a normal temperature

When a child is ill outside the home environment it is important to report any concerns to the appropriate people so that illness can be properly diagnosed.

At a nursery, school, or playgroup, the illness should be reported to a senior staff member who will decide whether to contact the child's parents/carers. A childminder or nanny should contact the parents direct.

It is important to keep a record of the child's symptoms, noting how they first appeared and how they have progressed as these may need to be passed on to the doctor and the parents.

When caring for a child who is unwell at school or nursery you may need to:

- Give practical help
- Provide reassurance
- Keep the child company
- Relax your normal expectations of the child

Information needed about each child in your care

Child care workers need to keep information about each child to enable contacts to be made in the case of an emergency.

Records should include:

- Child's full name and date of birth
- Child's address and telephone number
- Names and addresses of child's parents/carers
- Emergency contact telephone numbers
- Telephone numbers for the child's GP and health visitor

What to report to a doctor or carer if a child is ill:

- When you first noticed something was wrong
- What the symptoms were
- What action you took, e.g. taking the temperature
- How the symptoms have progressed

When giving medicines, always:

- Get the parent/carer's written consent first
- Only give medicines advised or prescribed by the child's GP or hospital doctor
- Follow the instructions for dosage and frequency carefully
- Store medicines carefully and safely, preferably in a locked cupboard
- Keep a record of medicines given, including dates and times

WORKING WITH PARENTS

If a child is ill, parents will need information and reassurance. The child care worker can help parents by:

- remaining calm
- giving parents accurate information
- reassuring parents that appropriate action has been taken
- showing understanding of parents' concerns
- offering support and practical help where possible

The parents of other children may need to know if another child in the setting has an infectious disease, so that they can take steps to ensure their child's health and well-being.

This information will need to be given while ensuring confidentiality, so it is important not to name children in these circumstances.

NOW ANSWER THESE QUESTIONS

1 What is a suitable temperature for a sick room?
2 Why is it important for a sick child to drink plenty of fluids?
3 What important points should you check when giving medicines to children?
4 What facts should you report to a doctor about a child who is ill?
5 What is a normal temperature in centigrade?

Child Safety and Health: Key Terms

You should now understand the following key terms. If you do not, go back through the previous chapter to find out.

ABC of resuscitation	Food intolerance	Preventive health
Accident book	Foreign body	Recovery position
Adult/child ratio	Gluten	Regression
Amino acid	Gross Motor	Rickets
Anaemia	Hand/eye co-ordination	Role model
Behavioural signs	HIB	Safe environment
Bronchodilator	Hygiene routines	Saturated fat
Carbohydrate	Immunisation	Screening
Child protection	Incomplete protein	Social skills
Complete protein	Indicator of neglect	Spread of infection
Cross-infection	Insulin	Toilet training
Dehydration	Koplik's spots	Tripod grasp
Designated person	Mineral	Unsaturated fat
Droplet infection	Otitis media	Vegan
Emergency procedure	Painful crisis	Water-borne infection
Emotional abuse	Palmar grasp	Water-soluble vitamin
'E' number	Parasite	Workplace policies and
Enzyme deficiency	Pathogen	procedures
Fat-soluble vitamin	Personal hygiene	
Fever	Physical abuse	
Fine motor	Pincer grasp	
First Aid	Positive role model	
Food additive	Potential hazard	

2 *LEARNING THROUGH PLAY*

Introduction

Children learn through play and this chapter provides an overview of play provision.

It includes the role of the adult in providing appropriate play, adapting materials and equipment to meet the needs of all children, clearing away and storing equipment. It also covers the effects of the physical environment including the room layout on the quality of play.

Providing a welcoming and reassuring environment will help children to feel comfortable and secure, able to take advantage of the activities on offer and to benefit from playing with other children. An attractive and stimulating environment helps children to learn and to value themselves and others – displaying children's work is an opportunity for them to participate in an educational and child-centred activity, sharing ideas and increasing intellectual and social skills.

Child care workers need to understand the role and value of play and the stages in play development. Children work hard at their play and increase their skills in all developmental areas as a result. Creative and physical play, role play, cooking with children, encouraging enjoyment in books and every other type of play provision require planning, preparation and delivery to make them accessible and attractive to children of different ages. This chapter will increase understanding of the purpose and potential of all play activities.

21 The Physical Environment

Successful child care requires a physical environment which is appropriate for children's needs. This may require adjustments and adaptations to the child care setting, which may not have been originally designed for this purpose.

ARRANGING THE AREA

Arrange furniture and equipment to make the setting as welcoming, reassuring and stimulating as possible for the children. When deciding how to arrange the area the following factors are important:

- **Safety requirements.** This includes heating, ventilation, lighting and Local Authority regulations. Exit doors should be securely fastened and doorways and fire escapes kept clear at all times. Staff should be aware of emergency procedures such as fire drills.
- **Security.** The setting should be geared to the needs of the children, with child-sized equipment, attractive displays and a quiet, calm atmosphere to help them feel comfortable and secure.
- **Layout.** Large spaces should be broken up and furniture arranged so as to create different areas for different types of activities e.g sand/water/painting/home corner/book area etc. This will discourage loud and aggressive behaviour, help to prevent accidents and encourage communication and learning.
- **Physical comfort.** Make sure that the temperature is 60–75⁰F, and keep a window open to help the air to circulate. Each area should be adequately lit, and the setting should include a quiet area with curtains or blinds, carpet and cushions where children can curl up with books or puzzles.
- **Flexibility.** The environment should allow children to work alone, with partners or in groups. A carpeted area is a good idea for bringing the children together for registration, sharing news or listening to stories. Smaller groups can be encouraged by putting out tables and chairs, and an area can also be provided for individual work such as reading to the carer or using the computer.

Group activities can be encouraged in a child-centred environment

- **Free movement.** Adults and children need to be able to access all parts of the setting. Planning must include plenty of space between activities and free access to the cloakroom, toilets, kitchen and outdoor areas.
- **Access to equipment.** Children thrive on responsibility and being allowed to make their own decisions within a safe framework. Resources should be as accessible as possible so that they can choose their own play materials.
- **Variety.** Child care workers will need to vary the activities on offer, perhaps with the help of the children, so access to storage areas will be necessary. Children can be encouraged to be responsible for parts of the setting by putting equipment away, keeping areas of the setting tidy, clearing litter from the outdoor area, helping to prepare snacks etc.

ENSURING ACCESSIBILITY

All activities and areas of the setting must be accessible to all children, regardless of their level of ability. Careful thought will need to be given to ensuring access for children with special needs. For example:

- Children with a **physical disability** may need wider doorways, ramps, a larger toilet area, extra space to manoeuvre around classroom furniture etc.
- **Hearing-impaired** children will require hearing aids, good lighting, use of British Sign Language etc.
- **Visually impaired** children will need large-print books, a richer and more varied range of tactile experiences etc. It will also be important to keep floors clear of obstructions and avoid changing the basic layout of furniture and fittings unnecessarily.

A child-oriented environment

There are several ways of making a home environment safer and more child-friendly:

- Small tables and chairs
- Small toilets/toilet seats
- Steps to make sinks etc. accessible and enable children to reach things
- Stair gates and fireguards
- High handles on doors
- Locks on cupboards, fridges and upstairs windows
- Low cupboards for storing creative equipment/books/activities for the children to choose.

THE NATURAL WORLD

Children enjoy and learn from activities involving growing plants and investigating the living world.

Gardening activities have many benefits for children if there is an awareness of their level of development and expectations are adjusted accordingly.

Benefits of gardening include:

- Increased knowledge of biological processes as seeds develop into plants
- Sense of achievement as plants grow
- Increased understanding of the needs of plants, e.g. for regular watering and feeding.
- Increased vocabulary, as children acquire new words to describe the plants, stages of their development and gardening activities

- Learning new skills, e.g. planting, digging, watering, pruning
- Enhanced awareness of time during the growth cycle
- Learning about safety issues, e.g. not eating berries or flowers, care with gardening tools, hygiene after gardening – washing hands etc.

Pets

There may also be an opportunity to keep pets in the child care setting. This can be an enjoyable way for children to learn about animals and to take responsibility for their care. However, it is important to make sure that no child or member of staff is allergic to any type of pet.

NOW ANSWER THESE QUESTIONS

1 What factors are important when deciding the layout of a child care setting?
2 What type of equipment would make the environment more child-orientated?
3 How can a child with a physical disability be made to feel welcome and secure in a child care setting?
4 How can the environment be adapted to enable a visually impaired child to make full use of all facilities?
5 What are the benefits of exploring the natural world for children?

A Stimulating Environment

Child care workers must be aware of how to provide a stimulating indoor and outdoor environment for the children in their care. They must be aware of the value of displaying children's work, the principles of display and have knowledge of a variety of techniques for displaying work.

PRINCIPLES OF DISPLAY

Displays should be easily accessible to children, so that they can investigate them and learn from them by looking, touching and feeling, smelling, tasting and hearing. This exploration via the five senses helps children to interact with their environment and stimulates their development.

- Displays should always show children's work and not adults'.
- Displays should be looked at, discussed and talked about and replaced frequently.
- Displays should be at the child's level so that they can be seen clearly and touched.
- Displays should be educational and child-centred (not just used to decorate bare walls).
- Parents, carers and visitors will be attracted to a well-positioned and well-presented display.

Think about the following:

- Where will the display be positioned? This will affect the size and type of display. A flat wall can be made into a three-dimensional display if there is enough space in front of it; a corner of a room can become a forest or a seabed or a space station; mobiles can be hung from the ceiling. A display can be on a table, on display screens, low cupboards, chests etc.
- Include some work from *all* the children. Always mount pictures for best effect and invite children to help choose, mount and display their work.
- When labelling children's work, use bright, clear letters in lower case, so that the children can read them. Include languages other than English if there are children whose first language is not English.

Displaying work encourages children's interest

Labelling in languages other than English reflects a multicultural society

Remember to reflect a multicultural, non-sexist society in the display. Reflect disabilities, age and men and women positively.

Interest tables and thematic displays encourage learning by stimulating exploration and questions.

- **Templates.** Use natural materials (like leaves and flowers), pinned to paper and sponged.
- **Silhouettes and borders.** Use colours that complement the main display. Encourage the children to make the borders.
- **Lettering.** Always use lower-case letters with a capital letter at the beginning. Writing should be clear and well-formed.
- **Mobile displays.** Hanging displays can be suspended from coat-hangers or similar objects. Small drawings/objects/paintings can also be displayed in this way.
- **Noticeboards.** Can be colourful and interesting. Try a border and mounting the notices using different types of print.
- **Display and interest tables.** These can be used to explore a theme or class topic, or to display work/collections from a recent outing. They should be used to display three-dimensional objects and located at child height in a quiet area where children can study them without distractions. The table should be covered and objects not to be touched placed in a protective container, e.g. a plastic tank.

The world around us

Seeing how things grow and develop is a vital part of learning about the world. Children can collect and display their findings – from autumn leaves to sea-life. Health and safety is important when displaying such objects. Be aware of the dangers of displaying poisonous berries and plants or sharp objects. Food should be fresh and changed regularly. Reference books should be available on the table for children to look up topics of interest.

Displays which appeal to children include the following:

- **Colour.** A co-ordinated backing and border to display the children's work to best advantage. Drapes add interest.

- **Texture.** Things that are interesting to touch and contrast with each other, e.g. smooth, shiny pebbles and rough sandpaper
- **Movement.** Hanging displays and windmills that spin in the breeze
- **Sound.** Crackly paper, shakers and musical instruments made by the children all make appealing displays.
- **Characters** that the children are familiar with from books read at storytime; people they have met on a trip, or who have visited the establishment.

Benefits to development:

- **Physical.** Development of fine motor skills through creative work, e.g. cutting, sticking, drawing, painting. Gross motor skills in co-ordination developed through reaching, stretching, bending, balancing.
- **Intellectual.** Stimulation of problem-solving skills, decision-making and thinking skills and memory.
- **Mathematical skills.** Increased awareness of pattern, shape, angles, measuring etc.
- **Language.** Acquisition of new words and vocabulary, use of reference books, development of discussion and listening skills, asking questions.
- **Emotional.** Enhanced sense of achievement and self-esteem. Children feel proud when their work is displayed for parents to see. Visual stimulus helps children to feel comfortable with their environment.
- **Social.** Encouragement of teamwork and co-operation between adults and children, sharing of resources and ideas. Opportunity to experience new materials and textures, sensory stimuli.
- **Cultural.** Increased awareness and knowledge of cultural diversity.

NOW ANSWER THESE QUESTIONS

1 What are the principles of good display?
2 Why is it important to display childrens' work?
3 What factors need consideration before planning a display?
4 What are the benefits of display to development?
5 Name some health and safety issues associated with displaying objects.

A Reassuring Environment

Child care workers need to provide a reassuring setting for the children in their care. Children will feel a greater sense of security and well-being if they know that their needs are met in a friendly and nurturing environment.

PROVIDING A SECURE ENVIRONMENT

In order to provide adequate and appropriate reassurance for children, knowledge of typical social/emotional development is necessary (see **Child Development,** pages 70–77. It is important to see the world from the child's point of view and to recognise the fears they may have, which can focus on separation, loud noises, the dark, spiders, strangers, animals or a host of other anxieties.

All children should be kept physically safe from harm, but they also need to feel safe and secure emotionally. It helps to adapt the physical environment (see pages 44-5) so that large areas are divided into smaller spaces for quieter activities. Pre-school children who are in day care should also be offered experiences which are similar to those they would have at home, e.g visiting the shops, the park, posting letters, sleep times and a daily routine.

It may be advisable to keep **comforters** labelled with the child's name and in a central location (see below). It can be useful to display a list of children's particular remedies or comforters in the staffroom.

It is important to see the world from the child's point of view

COMFORT

Children may show their fears by crying, clinging to their parent/carer, being unwilling to try new experiences, loss of appetite, sleeping problems etc. As children cannot always tell the adult what the source of their anxiety is, child carers must try to identify the cause.

How best to deal with the problem will depend on the cause of the anxiety. Some children may need more reassurance than you might expect in certain situations. Generally children will respond positively to:

- Clear and honest explanations about what is going to happen. These should be repeated frequently as young children may not remember.

- In the case of an unexpected incident, clear explanation of what has just happened
- A reassuring cuddle (but remember that not all children appreciate physical comfort)
- A stress-reducing activity like playdough, looking at books, painting

Many children have 'comfort objects' like a special blanket or soft toy – especially the under-two's. These should not be discouraged as they increase children's confidence and help them to develop independence.

All child care workers need to know how to reassure the children in their care. Comfort objects should be readily available.

A SENSE OF BELONGING

Children need to develop a sense of belonging. They will feel more at home in a setting that contains objects that are familiar to them from their homes and that reflect their culture:

- The home corner should contain a range of types of cooking equipment – woks, griddles, chop-sticks as well as saucepans, kettles, knives and forks.
- Dressing-up clothes should reflect a diversity of cultures and include saris, head-dresses, veils etc.
- Books should show positive images of different races, cultures and sexes and reflect equality of opportunity.
- Displays should promote a multicultural society, and children should be encouraged to produce art and/or written work about their homes and families for display.
- Visitors should be invited to come and talk to the children and help them to experience and appreciate social and cultural diversity.

- Coat hooks should be labelled with names and/or pictures.
- Equipment and resources should be personalised where possible – e.g. cups, flannels, work trays etc. should be named.

Children feel secure with familiar objects which reflect their own culture

OFFERING REASSURANCE

People who work with children must be warm, caring and responsive. Children easily detect those who appreciate and value their company, sometimes before you have spoken to them!

Always remember the following points when dealing with children:

- Be calm and quiet and try to speak softly.
- Maintain eye contact when speaking to children and try to meet them on their level – sit with them or squat down to them on the floor.
- Meet their needs quickly and effectively. Pick up the non-verbal clues and anticipate their needs – for example, the child hopping from foot to foot who needs the toilet!

- Be ready to cuddle a child who is unhappy or upset. Remember that failure to do so may harm their emotional development. On the other hand, *never* force physical contact on a child who does not welcome it.
- Encourage conversation and give children time to speak. Ask open-ended questions which cannot be answered with 'yes' or 'no', to encourage them to extend their use of language.
- Always be cheerful, positive and polite and enjoy your contact with all the children in your care.

NOW ANSWER THESE QUESTIONS

1 How can child care workers help children to feel secure?
2 What are some common fears in young children?
3 How can adults comfort children who are distressed?
4 What is a comfort object?
5 How can the home play area reflect cultural diversity?

24 The Importance of Play

Play is of great importance to children's development.

There are different theories about its importance and value. Play is now recognised as stimulating and encouraging growth in every developmental area, enabling children to acquire and practise many skills and to explore their physical and social environment. As children grow and develop, they pass through recognisable stages of play. There are many different types of play and they have close links with different aspects of children's learning.

The play environment includes the physical setting, the objects that are provided within it to encourage play, how they are set out, and the adults within it who enable and encourage play.

THEORIES ABOUT PLAY

Play stimulates growth in every developmental area

There are different views about the role and value of play.

1   An old-fashioned view is that it is simply a way of passing time and keeping children occupied until they can go to work.

2   **Piaget** argued that play enables a child to develop ways of thinking. This learning goes through three main stages:

i)   In the first two years, during the sensory motor stage, play enables children to explore and manipulate their environment to see how they can master it.

ii) Between two and seven years ('the pre-operational stage') children's symbolic or make-believe play reflects their broadening experience and imagination.

iii) From seven years on (the 'concrete operations stage') children play using rules and become truly sociable.

3   According to social learning theorists, including Bandura, children learn by using play to model their ideas and behaviour on the people they see around them.

4   Psychoanalysts, including Freud, believe that the main value of play is to help children to overcome potential problems in relation-ships with others.

All of these theories contain an element of truth. Play can also been seen as children's 'work'. It enables them to learn how to deal with people, objects and themselves by 'doing'. It is also enjoyable, repetitive, and non-threat-ening.

24

PLAY AND DEVELOPMENT

Play stimulates growth in every developmental area:

- **Physically** it encourages movement and control in gross and fine motor skills.
- **Intellectually** it leads to the development of thinking and learning, including conceptual thought, problem-solving, creativity, imagination, memory and concentration.
- **Linguistically** play stimulates the development of verbal and non-verbal communication skills.

- **Emotionally** play provides the opportunity to experience and express a range of emotions, and to learn how to control them.
- **Socially** play enables children to develop the skills they need for interaction with others. This includes learning to share, co-operate, take turns and make friends.
- **Morally** play helps children to learn the existence of rules, and how to conform to them. Through play they can gain a sense of what is right or wrong and develop a conscience.

THE STAGES OF PLAY

Social play (i.e. the ability to play with others) develops as children mature.

The stages can usually be observed around the following ages:

AGE	PLAY	DESCRIPTION
0–2 years	Solitary	Playing alone, often very inventively with objects, exploring and experimenting
2–3 years	Parallel	Playing at personal activity alongside another child but not interacting with them
3 years onwards	Associative	Intermittent communication and interaction with another child, maybe at the same activity, but still personal play
3 years onwards	Co-operative	Child is able to take account of others actions and needs to co-operate by taking on a role in a group.

TYPES OF PLAY

Play can be divided into different types which may overlap in a single activity:

- **Manipulative:** requiring skill in hand-eye co-ordination including drawing and writing
- **Specific:** designed to instruct, involving a specific task, e.g. jigsaws.

- **Exploratory:** involving creativity, finding out how things work and what happens to them, construction or destruction
- **Symbolic:** 'pretend' and imaginative play, laying a foundation for conceptual thought

NOW ANSWER THESE QUESTIONS

1 What are some of the main ideas about the value of play?
2 Why is play important to development?
3 How does play encourage social development?
4 Name the four stages of social play.
5 What are the different types of play?

25 The Adult's Role

Adults have an essential role to play in the provision and support of children's learning and play. Adult child care workers should have a good understanding of development and how to meet children's needs at different stages. They need to know how to provide a safe and secure play environment and when and how to intervene in children's play.

SUPPORTING CHILDREN'S LEARNING

Many activities in a child care environment are provided and directed by adults. Adults should have a knowledge and understanding of how children learn in order to provide activities that are suitable for their age and stage of development. It is vital that any materials provided to support children's learning are adapted to meet any particular needs a child may have at any stage in their development.

All children, including those with special needs, should be given the opportunity to develop skills of independence, self-reliance and self-confidence.

Piaget's stages of intellectual development can help workers to make appropriate provision for children at different ages:

AGE	CHILDREN'S DEVELOPMENT	ADULT'S ROLE
0–2 years: the **Sensory Motor** stage	Children build up a mental picture of the things around them based on their sensory contact with their environment and the objects in it. They do this when they hold, feel, suck, listen to, look at, shake and throw things. By the time they are one year old, babies learn that objects exist even if they cannot see them.	Give children new experiences and objects to explore using all their senses.
2–7 years: the **Pre-operations** stage	Children's thought processes are developing, but they are not fully logical. They begin to use symbols to stand for something else. This allows the growth of their imagination. They show a high degree of egocentricity (self-centredness) during this stage.	Provide materials and the environment for imaginative play. Direct and structure activities or support those that are initiated by children by encouraging and helping them when appropriate.
7–11 years: the **Concrete Operations** stage	Children's learning becomes more rational and mature. In the initial stage (Concrete Operations) children can only think logically if they are able to manipulate the objects they are thinking about.	Provide tools and materials that are appropriate to the initial stage. In the following stage (**Formal Operations**), children can manipulate their own thoughts and therefore do not need objects to help them (e.g. they can do mental arithmetic). Adults can enhance children's learning by discussion and encouragement.

25

THE PLAY ENVIRONMENT

The physical environment for play should be planned and equipped to ensure that children are safe, secure, happy and stimulated. This is best achieved if the scale of the building, the furniture and the outdoor area suit the size of the children. Children with impaired mobility should be able to move around easily.

Access points must be left clear and equipment positioned in places that best suit their use. This means that, for example, quiet activities should be positioned away from noisy or physical activities, messy activities should be near a sink etc. The environment must be clean and hygienic and equipment checked regularly for damage and wear.

Good storage is important because, if provided at the children's height and labelled clearly, it can increase access to play materials and encourage children's independence in using them. It also helps if children are involved in the clearing away of play materials after use.

The role of the adult in providing for play

Adults have an important role in providing for and stimulating children's play. They should be involved in planning, preparation and support and in making best use of the opportunities play provides to stimulate children's development. They can do this by interacting appropriately during the activity and observing and monitoring what is happening.

ADULT ROLE	WHAT THIS INCLUDES
Planning	Meeting the requirements of the National Curriculum or enabling the attainment of desirable outcomes. Being aware of the developmental level and skills of the group, including any special needs. Knowing what will be enjoyable, reflect cultural diversity, and match any current curriculum theme. Understanding the limitations of the physical environment and the need for safety.
Preparation	Gathering the necessary equipment, arranging it in an appropriate position and presenting it in attractive manner
Interaction	Participation as an adult can mean joining in, playing alongside, commenting on the play, offering advice and making suggestions. In some situations intervention may only be required if children appeal for help, cannot solve problems unaided, or when there is disruption, danger, interference or unresolved difficulties. In other cases adults may participate as equals, taking a role within the play situation but at the same time being able to withdraw without disrupting it.
Observation and monitoring	Observing how an activity is used and whether it is appropriate for the children, enabling adult providers to modify or change an activity for future use or to extend the children's use of it.

NOW ANSWER THESE QUESTIONS

1   What knowledge do adults need in order to provide suitable activities for children?
2   What are the three stages of children's learning according to Piaget?
3   Name three essentials when planning the play environment.
4   Name five key aspects of the adult's role when providing play.
5   Why is planning for play essential?

26 Communication, Books and Music

Effective communication between adults and children is essential for children's growth and development. It is the channel through which ideas, facts and feelings are conveyed. Stories, books and music can be used to encourage communication. They should be chosen at a level that is appropriate to the children's development and presented in a way that encourages participation, attention and enjoyment.

THE IMPORTANCE OF COMMUNICATION

Communication is vital to children's development. It usually involves both:

- **Verbal** communication, including talking and listening, singing and reading
- **Non-verbal** communication, including 'body language', facial expression, gesture and eye contact

The effective use of language is essential in order for people to be able to function well within society. It also satisfies the human need to communicate feelings, needs, ideas and thoughts. Communication involving talking and listening activities will stimulate a child's language development. When speaking to children always:

- Use the appropriate speed and tone of voice
- Speak clearly and calmly.
- Use open-ended questions. These require several words in reply rather than simply 'yes' or 'no' in response to a closed question.
- Talk about a range of subjects in a variety of ways.

Language diversity should be valued in all child care establishments. It can be promoted through the use of signs, books, songs and displays in a variety of languages, including sign language.

Communication difficulties can arise if children have inadequate contact with adult carers or if they have impairments that impede communication. These children may need special programmes to meet their individual and special needs.

Language satisfies the human need to communicate feelings, needs, thoughts and ideas

STORIES AND BOOKS

Stories and books are of great value when used with young children. They can be used to promote:

- **Language skills** through seeing and hearing different patterns of speech and a range of vocabulary. They will also lay the foundation for reading and writing.
- **Intellectual development** through stimulating thoughts and ideas, promoting concentration and conceptual thought

- **Emotional development** through exposing the child to a range of feelings that they can learn to recognise and empathise with and understand and learn to deal with
- **Social skills**, both through exposure to a range of different behaviours in stories, and the social experience of listening with a group or individually with an adult

When choosing books to read or setting out a book area for children, the key priorities are as follows:

- The books should be of the right level and length for the age and stage of development of the children.
- There should be a wide range of books. Select a variety of books that will engage and maintain children's interest, including books with stories, pictures, poetry and rhymes, facts, interest, and books which are relevant to the children's own experiences. Picture books and those with a limited text are more suitable for younger children. The use of repetition is also important for younger children. Children gradually learn to appreciate more complex pictures and text. By infant school age, they enjoy more complex stories that reflect their wider interests and greater concentration skills.
- The books should reflect positive images of all people in society, including women and men, disabled people and those of different cultural, racial and social origins.
- Bookshelves should be accessible and at child height. Books should be in an area where they can be read in comfort, free from the distraction of other activities.

Reading books and telling stories

Having chosen an appropriate book to read or story to tell, it is very useful to:

- Familiarise yourself with the story and any rhymes or songs that go with it
- Collect or make any visual aids that you will use to illustrate the story
- Choose the setting where you will tell it, ensuring that it is comfortable and free from distractions

When reading the book or telling a story, remember to:

- Engage the interest of the children to start with, by introducing it in a way that will enable them to identify with the story.
- Maintain their interest by using different tones of voice, varying the pace at which you speak, showing them that you are enjoying the story, showing them the book as you are reading it (this may involve turning it round if you are sitting facing the children), and using visual aids.
- Extend their interest and enjoyment by discussing the story, asking questions, singing songs and saying rhymes.

COMMUNICATION THROUGH THE USE OF MUSIC

Music can be used in a variety of forms to help communication with young children. It is not only enjoyable in itself, but can cut across other barriers to communication such as language differences, delay, impairments etc.

When using music with children it is important to:

- Choose appropriate music and songs, using familiar as well as new ones

- Become familiar with them in advance in order to play or sing them and engage the children's attention
- Give children the opportunity to choose their own songs
- Choose music and songs that reflect a variety of cultures and languages
- Allow the children to use musical instruments and to make their own instruments and sounds

NOW ANSWER THESE QUESTIONS

1 What are the two main aspects of communication?
2 How can language diversity be valued and encouraged in a child care establishment?
3 What are the benefits of using stories and books with children?
4 Name five different types of books.
5 How can music help communication?

27 Role Play, Cooking and Playing Games

Role play involves children taking on and acting out the roles of people around them. Cooking activities can involve both hot and cold ingredients and a variety of tasks and recipes. Table-top and physical games can be very enjoyable for young children. All these activities can stimulate all-round development and sensory awareness, and there are useful principles to consider when providing for them.

THE VALUE OF ROLE PLAY

Role play involves both imaginative and imitative play. Infants first copy adult actions and then their use of tools and equipment. In the right conditions children between two and three years appear to begin role play spontaneously. They start by imitating the people in their families who are close to them and then from about three onwards they extend this to less familiar adults who they may meet either in real life or the media.

Role play is of great significance to the all-round development of the child. In particular, it enables children to:

Play is a positive self-image builder

- Explore and understand how other people behave
- Explore the feelings of others in a range of different situations
- Act out their own feelings and relationships in a safe way
- Rehearse roles they have not yet taken on in real life
- Increase their manipulative skills, develop concepts and other intellectual skills, and enhance their social and emotional skills
- Extend their awareness of other people including those from other cultural groups

Providing for role play

Adults can provide a range of equipment and situations to stimulate role play:

- Young children can use dolls to act out the roles of familiar carers
- As they develop, children enjoy using dressing up clothes and hats to enhance their role play
- In a nursery environment an imaginative play area can be provided which can serve as a range of different environments

including home, shop or place of work. Clothes and implements can also be provided, reflecting a range of different cultures. The area should be arranged so that all children can participate, including those with physical impairments.

- A range of equipment based on different themes can be provided to stimulate children's role play. This can prompt them to explore situations which may be new, familiar or based on fantasy.
- Models of people, puppets, and other objects can also be used to stimulate play.
- Both real tools and 'pretend' equipment can be provided (always bearing in mind health and safety factors).

Adults need to be very sensitive in their intervention during role play to avoid interrupting any fantasy that children are creating. They may however be instrumental in extending children's play by participating, if invited, as equal partners. In this way they can extend children's language and vocabulary, conceptual thought and expression of feelings and ideas.

PROVIDING FOR A COOKING ACTIVITY

Cooking is an ideal activity because it stimulates all the senses and each area of development. When planning cooking activities, take into account the following:

- **Hygiene.** Requirements include having clean hands, wearing clean protective clothing, tying hair, using clean implements and storing food at correct temperatures.
- **Safety.** This must be carefully considered in relation to the age of the children. Special care is needed when dealing with hot liquids, sharp cooking implements and spillages. Cooking processes can involve both hot and cold ingredients. The use of cold recipes will reduce health and safety risks for younger children.
- **Healthy eating.** This is an important factor when choosing food and recipes. Always consider different food values and the importance of a balanced diet.
- **Cultural diversity.** Cooking activities are an ideal opportunity to introduce foods from other cultures to the majority group in a setting. The self-esteem of children from minority cultural groups will be enhanced by the use of food that is familiar to them.
- **Special needs.** Children can be involved in the entire process according to their age, development and needs. The choice of recipe and processes should be adapted to suit children with special needs so that they can participate as fully as possible.

PLAYING GAMES WITH CHILDREN

Table-top games can be of great value in increasing children's concept of number and their matching, sequencing and concentration skills. The experience of being part of a group, sharing, taking turns and showing consideration for others also aids social development.

Playing games in a controlled environment, with adult assistance, allows children to learn how to cope emotionally with the experience of winning and losing. Physical games can also be very enjoyable for young children.

When providing games the following factors should be considered:

- The **age and stage of development** of the child. Younger children may not be able to share, co-operate or take turns with other children and need games that they can play with an adult supervising, such as dominoes or other matching games. The ability to play games with other children comes gradually. From three years onwards, children develop more social skills and become better at understanding the rules and the point of games. This enables them to play a range of games of increasing complexity. Physical games like oranges and lemons can be very enjoyable for young children.
- **Special needs.** It may be necessary to adapt games for children who have special physical or intellectual needs.
- **Winning and losing.** Most children find losing difficult, and the repeated experience of losing can be a blow to some children's self-esteem. Children can be helped by discussion and by playing games where everyone has a chance of winning at some time. It is useful to emphasise the importance and enjoyment of taking part rather than winning. Non-competitive games that involve team co-operation and emphasise completing an activity rather than winning also help to reduce the pain of losing.

NOW ANSWER THESE QUESTIONS

1. What does role play involve and why is it of value?
2. What can an imaginative play area be turned into?
3. What other materials can be provided to stimulate role play?
4. Why can cooking activities be of value to children?
5. Why is playing games with children of value?

Creative Play and Objects of Interest

Creative play involves children bringing something into existence. It encourages all developmental areas and sensory awareness. Natural and manufactured materials can be used both for creative play and as objects of interest which can be explored and displayed in their own right. Child care workers need to understand the principles underlying the effective provision of creative play and have an awareness of the health and safety issues involved.

CREATIVE PLAY

To create is to bring into existence. Creative play involves children choosing from materials, usually provided by adults, and using their skill and imagination to make something original and new. It includes experimentation and exploration of natural and manufactured materials. If children are given a wide range of materials they will be more likely to create something different. Health and safety issues must always be addressed when providing materials.

Sand can be used wet or dry in a number of ways

Creativity and development

Creative play can be used to enhance all areas of development and to stimulate sensory awareness:

- Creativity is an expressive form of play enabling children to express and deal with what they are feeling and thinking.
- It is experiential and stimulates the senses, especially those of touch and sight, and the imagination.
- It encourages the development of fine motor skills through the use of tools and implements.
- It stimulates social development through sharing resources and taking turns.

Principles of providing for creativity

When providing for creative play adults should consider the following principles:

- To avoid frustration, children need materials and tools which are appropriate to their stage of development, the right size and enjoyable to use.
- The contribution of creative activity to other areas of learning should be considered.
- Emphasis should be placed on the creative process rather than the end-product of the activity.
- All the children in a group should be able to participate, including those with special needs.
- Health and safety factors must always be considered.

MATERIALS FOR CREATIVE PLAY

These can be divided into **natural** and **manufactured** materials. Both have their inherent advantages and disadvantages.

The table opposite shows the different types of manufactured and natural materials, and the issues involved in their use.

MATERIAL	POSITIVES	ISSUES
Natural Water	Familiar, enjoyable, absorbing, cheap, readily available, therapeutic, can be used with many different implements and additions	Exacerbates some skin conditions, spilling can be hazardous, clothing needs protection.
Sand	Can be used wet or dry in a variety of ways, inexpensive and available, enjoyable, relaxing, therapeutic, less familiar	Not all types suitable for play, must be kept clean, can get in eyes and hair, spilling can be hazardous.
Malleable foodstuffs	Clay and dough can be used many times, with many different tools and implements; are readily available, soothing, pleasurable. Peas, beans, lentils and pasta provide different textures, shapes and colours and are easy to handle.	Health issues concerning freshness when stored, safety if eaten, protection of clothing. Ethical issues over use of food, especially if not past 'sell-by' date, possible allergies need consideration.
Plants and wood	Fresh or dried leaves, berries and flowers, wood, bark are readily available; children enjoy collecting them; a stimulus for learning and aesthetic awareness	Poisonous plant material must not be used, storage needs care.
Manufactured Paint	Can be used in many ways with fingers or tools, helps manipulative skills, gives a sense of pride and achievement, valuable for expression, enjoyable	Must be non-toxic, protection of clothing and surfaces, emphasis on outcomes and interpretation to be avoided.
Pencils, crayons and drawing materials	Encourage concentration, experimentation and expression. Materials can be used in combination with each other, different sizes readily available, inexpensive, easily stored and made available for use	Must be non-toxic, sharp points need careful use.
Collage and construction	Paper, magazines, material, wool, cards, boxes, food containers and other discarded materials are ideal for two- or three-dimensional outcomes. Stimulates ideas, designs, technology. Very enjoyable, stimulates fine motor skills.	Health and hygiene, storage, accessibility to children, frustration if tools are inadequate for the task.

NOW ANSWER THESE QUESTIONS

1 How can creative activities stimulate development?
2 What issues should you particularly consider when providing for creative play?
3 What are the two main types of materials that can be provided for creative play?
4 Name some materials that can be used for creative play.
5 What are the main health and safety issues to be considered when providing materials and objects of interest?

29 Physical and Manipulative Play

Physical play encourages the growth, development and control of bodily movements. Physical development includes gross motor skills that involve whole-body and limb movements. It also includes gross and fine manipulative skills involving the whole hand or finger and thumb movements, together with hand-eye co-ordination.

A range of equipment is available to stimulate children's physical development. This must be provided according to the age and stage of development of the children and with careful attention to health and safety.

PHYSICAL PLAY AND DEVELOPMENT

Physical play helps children to gain control over their bodies by allowing them to repeat and practise physical skills. It stimulates healthy growth and development. It enables children to gain co-ordination, muscle control and strength, balance and agility; to learn gross motor skills including how to run, jump, hop, skip, crawl, climb, balance, pull, push, lift, throw, catch, pedal, steer and to discriminate between speed and distance. It helps them to gain confidence, to experience pleasure, a sense of freedom and less restriction in their play, and to develop sensory awareness.

Principles of providing for physical play

- Materials should be appropriate to the stage of development of the child. If they do not present a challenge, the child will learn nothing new and may become bored, but if they are too difficult to use, the child may become frustrated and stop trying.
- Equipment needs to be set up safely, imaginatively and in an appropriate place where it does not interfere with other activities.
- Equipment should be at a suitable level for the age and size of the children who use it, and include provision for children with physical impairments.
- Different areas for different ages may be advisable.
- Supervision is needed according to the age and skill of the children. They may need encouragement to use or share equipment and to attempt new challenges.
- A change of clothing may be advisable, especially in the case of outdoor play.

FUNCTION	EQUIPMENT	ISSUES
Climbing, balancing, swinging	Climbing frame, planks, ladders, A-frames, slides, swings	Must match size of the children, supervision needed, must be erected safely and checked for damage and wear, care needed when moving and storing
Jumping, crawling	Tyres, crates, boxes, trampolines, pipes, tunnels	Supervision needed
Pushing, pulling, moving	Trolleys, bikes, scooters, prams, pushchairs, carts,	Storage, maintenance
Throwing, catching	Balls, hoops, quoits, bats, beanbags	Adult intervention helpful
Running, moving	Open space indoors or outside	Secure boundaries help supervision, health and safety

MANIPULATIVE PLAY

Manipulative play involves using the hands – either the whole hand in gross manipulative skills, or the fingers and thumbs of the hands used independently in fine manipulative skills. It is important for children to develop manipulative skills and to co-ordinate their eye movements with them. These skills are necessary as a foundation for the use of tools that underpin learning in many areas – for example, using pencils and books, and the skills that bring personal independence.

Principles of providing for manipulative play

- Provide a range of attractive materials that are appropriate to the stage of development of the child. If materials present no challenge the child will learn nothing new and may become bored; if they are too difficult to use, the child may become frustrated, stop trying, and learn little.
- Provide sufficient space for the activity.
- Position the equipment so that it is safe, attractive, allows choice and there is sufficient space to encourage the children to develop the activity.
- Make sure surfaces are safe and the equipment is hygienic, safe and checked for defects.
- Make sure that supervision is appropriate to the equipment being used and sufficient to ensure children's safety.

MATERIALS FOR MANIPULATIVE PLAY

The following development stages help to indicate a range of different objects suitable to provide for a child.

1   Babies use their hands to explore objects. By six months they are fascinated by small toys within reach, grab them with their whole hand using a palmar grasp, transfer them from hand to hand and put them in their mouth to explore them. By nine months they can use an **inferior pincer grasp** with index finger and thumb, hold two objects and bang them together. By one year they can use a **mature pincer grasp** and release objects, and also a primitive **tripod grasp** using the thumb and first two fingers. A range of small, safe objects and toys as well as activity centres will stimulate babies at this age.

2   Between the ages of one and two, children learn to use a **palmar** then a tripod grasp to hold crayons, books, a spoon, to post objects through small spaces, to build a tower of bricks and to attempt to thread beads. Toys of this kind will stimulate development.

3   From two to three years, children can hold a pencil in their preferred hand, draw circles, lines and dots, use a pincer grasp to pick up and put down tiny toys, and use a fine pincer grasp with both hands to do complicated tasks including turning the pages of a book one at a time.

4   At three years the child can cut with scissors, paint with a large brush and thread wooden beads on a large shoelace.

5   At four years the child can grasp a pencil maturely, draw and thread smaller beads. They can also catch, throw and bounce a ball and hit it with a bat.

6   Between five and seven years fine manipulative skills become more and more co-ordinated and controlled, enabling children to write, draw, cut, thread, sew, and build. They are also able to play a variety of ball games.

NOW ANSWER THESE QUESTIONS

1   What does physical play enable a child to do?
2   What are some of the issues to consider when providing for physical play ?
3   Suggest some equipment that can be used for physical play.
4   What are some of the issues to consider when providing for manipulative play?
5   What are the key factors to consider when providing equipment for manipulative play?

Learning Through Play: Key Terms

You should now understand the following key terms. If you do not, go back through the previous chapter to find out.

Anti-discriminatory environment
Associative play
Child-centred
Collage
Conceptual thought
Co-operative play
Creative play
Display techniques
Egocentric
Imaginative play
Imitative play
Impairments

Interaction
Interest tables
Intervention
Language diversity
Malleable materials
Manipulative play
Monitoring
Multicultural society
Natural and manufactured materials
Non-verbal communication
Observation

Parallel play
Piaget
Role play
Sensory Motor stage
Solitary play
Symbolic play
Theories

3 A POSITIVE ENVIRONMENT

Introduction

This chapter aims to increase understanding about attitudes, discrimination and how to provide equality of opportunity to all children regardless of their race, gender, religion or disability.

It is the responsibility of child care workers to provide a positive environment that recognises, accommodates and embraces differences between people and provides positive images of all children.

Such an approach will encourage healthy emotional and social development and encourage a positive self-image. Knowledge of the sequence and rate of development will help you to understand how to meet children's needs appropriately. Child care workers need to understand why children behave as they do and what influences their actions and reactions. This will help in the development of a framework for behaviour and the management of unwanted behaviour if and when it occurs.

Working in partnership with parents/carers is essential to promote the best interests of the child. This includes communicating effectively, respecting parents' views and recognising their knowledge and expertise. Understanding the early years services provided by statutory, voluntary and private organisations will enable child care and education workers to help carers make the best use of the services that are available to them and their children.

Attitudes and Discrimination

It is important to adopt positive attitudes when working with children and their families. Negative attitudes and assumptions based on stereotypical ideas about people can damage children's personal development and lead to discriminatory practices against them. These result in reduced chances and achievements in later life.

POSITIVE AND NEGATIVE ATTITUDES

Attitudes are the opinions and ways of thinking that we have. Our attitude to people affects the way we act and behave towards them. Attitudes can be positive or negative.

A **positive** attitude towards a person based on knowledge, understanding and respect enables that person to feel good, valued, and have high self-esteem.

Negative attitudes are based on poorly informed and stereotypical images

A **negative** attitude towards a person, based on poorly informed opinion and stereotypical assumptions, can lead to low self-esteem and feeling unwanted or rejected.

Positive attitudes are therefore very important when working with children and their families. Child care workers need to examine their attitudes to make sure that they are not based on any negative or stereotypical assumptions.

Assumptions

To **assume** is to believe something without evidence or proof. Making assumptions can be a very useful way of helping to understand the world around us. Assumptions enable us to predict what is going to happen and to feel secure. Children gain security from assuming many things. For example, if it is home time, a child will assume that a carer will be meeting them; if it is bedtime, they will assume that an adult will read them a story; if they are hurt, they will assume that an adult will be there to help them etc. Such assumptions give a positive framework to their lives.

Stereotyping, however, involves assuming that all the people who share one characteristic (e.g. the same gender, race, or social origin) also share another set of character-istics (e.g. being less strong, less able).

We give specific names to some forms of negative attitudes and assumptions:

- **Racism,** when people of one race or culture believe they are superior to another
- **Sexism,** when people of one gender believe they are superior to the other

Other forms of stereotyping have less specific names. They involve discrimination against people with disabilities, those in low socio-economic groups, those of differing sexual orientation and others.

Negative stereotypical assumptions can be very harmful. They are assumptions based on incomplete knowledge and understanding and on fixed and prejudicial attitudes.

Discrimination

Stereotyping can lead to:

- **Discrimination** (i.e. unfavourable treatment of people based on prejudice)
- **Oppression** (using power to dominate and reduce people's life chances)

When one group in society is more powerful than another group and hold stereotypical attitudes, they can block the progress of other members of society. This reduces that group's life chances and achievements.

Discrimination occurs not only when one person behaves in an oppressive manner towards another. It can also occur when individual workers have positive attitudes, but the institution is not organised to meet the needs of all the people within it, or even excludes some people from membership altogether. This can happen when, for example:

- Children with impairments are not provided with the equipment they need to enter or to take a full part in the curriculum
- The needs of children from minority religious groups are not recognised
- Activities are organised in a way that makes it difficult for some children to participate

This is called **institutionalised discrimination**. While most child workers try to ensure that they have positive attitudes, they are sometimes less aware of institutionalised practices that discriminate against certain groups of children and parents.

EFFECTS OF DISCRIMINATION

Discrimination can affect individuals and groups within any child care setting. These are some of the main groups affected:

- Disabled children and their families are prone to many forms of obvious discrimination. Even in a caring environment, concern to meet their special needs can distract from meeting their ordinary needs and from seeing them as unique individuals. Enabling people with disabilities to take an effective part in the world is called **empowerment.**

- In a predominantly white society, children from black and other ethnic groups often experience overt racist comments and treatment. It is difficult to learn in an environment where such practices are allowed to exist. Racism is sometimes covert and involves, for example, a lack of under-standing of differences, a lack of positive images of black people, or an absence of equipment and resources that reflect a multicultural society. Racism discourages the growth of the individual and prevents children reaching their full potential.

- There is evidence to show that women are still discriminated against. Most top job positions are filled by men; women are more often employed in low-status jobs. Much has been done to address gender bias in schools, but certain attitudes and assumptions continue to cause many women to under-achieve.

- Children from lower socio-economic groups continue to under-achieve academically. The introduction of comprehensive education has given opportunity to all individuals, but it has failed to address the causes of under-achievement linked to social class.

NOW ANSWER THESE QUESTIONS

1. Why is it important to have a positive attitude when working with children?
2. What is negative stereotyping?
3. What is discrimination?
4. Why can institutionalised discrimination occur even if workers have positive attitudes?
5. Who are the main groups affected by discrimination?

31

Promoting Equality

Equality of opportunity is about recognising differences and enabling people to have the opportunity to participate in every area of life to the best of their abilities. It can be promoted at government level by the passing of laws, at institutional level through working practices and codes of conduct, and at a personal level through increased awareness and skills in meeting needs.

WHAT IS EQUALITY?

Promoting equality means enabling people to have an equal chance of participating in life

Promoting equality of opportunity means enabling people to have an equal chance of participating in life to the best of their abilities, whatever their gender, race, religion, disability or social background. This includes providing equal access to education, health, social services and jobs.

Equality of opportunity is not about treating all people the same and ignoring differences. Ignoring differences can be the very reason that people are *not* given equality of opportunity – because their needs are not recognised.

For example, if three candidates are invited for an interview on the first floor of a building that does not have a lift, and one candidate uses a wheelchair, that person would not have an equal opportunity to get the job.

Other examples of ignoring differences may be less obvious but the effects are no less detrimental. For example, not recognising that some families cannot afford to pay for school outings; that some religious groups have dress and dietary requirements; that one gender group may dominate particular activities or curriculum areas – all these failures to recognise difference would have a serious adverse effect on the people concerned.

People are not the same: they have many differences and their individual and particular needs need to be recognised and accommodated. There is now a commitment at many levels of society to promote equality of opportunity and to combat oppression and discrimination.

AT GOVERNMENT LEVEL

The promotion of equality of opportunity is possible at a number of different levels in society. At government level, laws have been passed in Parliament aimed at combatting some forms of oppression and discrimination.

Some people believe that passing laws does not stop discrimination, and that discrimination will still exist. This may be true, but a law does make a public statement about what is not acceptable in society and gives those in authority the power to penalise those who break it. Few people would want to make

housebreaking legal just because the law does not stop it from happening.

Laws on disability

- The Education Act 1944 placed a general duty on LEAs to provide education for all children, including those with special needs.
- The Disabled Persons (Employment) Act 1944 required employers to engage a certain proportion of disabled employees.
- The Education Act 1981 is the main piece of legislation regarding special education. It

lays down specific procedures for the assessment and statementing of children.

- The Education Reform Act 1988 required LEAs to provide access to the National Curriculum for all children including those with special needs, and to identify and assess their needs.
- The Chronically Sick and Disabled Person's Act 1970 and the Disabled Persons Act 1986 imposed various duties on local authorities towards disabled people, including identifying the numbers of disabled people, providing a number of services and publishing information about them.
- The Children Act 1989 defined the services that should be provided by a local authority for 'children in need' in their area, including those who are disabled.
- The Disability Discrimination Act 1995 was passed to ensure that any services offered to the public in general must be accessible to people with disabilities.

Race legislation

The Race Relations Act 1965 outlawed discrimination on the basis of race in the provision of goods or services to the public, or in employment or housing. It also became illegal to incite racial hatred. The Race Relations Board was set up to investigate complaints of racial discrimination but had little power. In 1976 the Commission for Racial Equality (now the REC) was given power to take people to court for racial discrimination.

Gender legislation

- The Equal Pay Act 1970 gave women the right to equal pay to men for equal work.
- The Employment Protection Act 1975 gave women the right to paid maternity leave.
- The Sex Discrimination Act 1975 outlawed discrimination on the grounds of sex in employment, education, provision of goods and services and housing.
- The Equal Opportunities Commission was set up in 1975 to enforce the laws relating to discrimination.

AT INSTITUTIONAL LEVEL

Many organisations now adopt a voluntary equal opportunities policy in their recruitment procedures. You will see a statement of this commitment on many job advertisements.

Many also have a written code of practice clearly stating that no child or adult will receive less favourable treatment on the grounds of gender, race, religion, disability or other factors.

Within some establishments resources and staffing are provided to ensure greater equality of opportunity.

It is recognised by many institutions and establishments that there is a need to regularly review and evaluate provision and policy to ensure that practices are up to date and in line with current understanding of the issues.

AT A PERSONAL LEVEL

At a personal level people can:

- Examine their own attitudes and practices
- Increase their knowledge and understanding of people who are different from themselves

- Undertake training and awareness raising courses to increase their ability to provide for the needs of all
- Always be looking for up to date information and resources

NOW ANSWER THESE QUESTIONS

1 What do you understand by the phrase 'equality of opportunity'?
2 What is wrong with treating everyone the same?
3 In which three areas have most equal opportunities laws been passed?
4 How can establishments promote equality of opportunity?
5 What can you do on a personal level to promote equality of opportunity?

32

Providing for Equality

Understanding and acceptance of family diversity is essential for child care workers. All children can benefit from an environment that embraces cultural and linguistic diversity. Discrimination must be actively opposed. A positive working environment is achieved primarily through attitudes and behaviour and enhanced by the provision of resources.

VALUING DIVERSITY

Acceptance of family diversity and the different childcare practices it produces is essential for child care workers if they are to adopt an anti-discriminatory approach to their work.

People tend to see the world from their own point of view. We begin with an awareness of ourselves and then come to understand others. For this reason we often think of ourselves and our immediate environment as 'normal' and things that are different and outside it as 'not quite normal'. This view is not always helpful or professional when working with children and their families.

Cultural differences are more likely to be understood and valued in a child care environment where difference is seen as a positive quality to be valued

Families have many differences. They vary in their beliefs and ways of behaving, in their size, structure, wealth and physical resources. Different types of families can and do provide security for their children and foster their healthy development in different ways. Families should be accepted, respected and valued for the care they give their children. Differences in style should not be judged as better or worse. Workers need to develop an understanding of different practices.

Difficulties in caring for children, or failure to meet their needs, and the disadvantages that some children experience as a result, are not caused by the obvious differences between families. They are more closely linked to the personal resources, abilities and attitudes that exist within a family group.

Valuing cultural diversity

All children can benefit from an environment that embraces cultural and linguistic diversity. Cultural differences are more likely to be valued and understood in a child care

environment where difference is seen as a positive quality to be valued. Children in modern society come from a variety of cultural backgrounds. They are more likely to experience equality of opportunity and feel valued in a positive environment where their cultures are recognised and reflected in the provision of books and resources for their use. In schools and nurseries where there is less diversity of background, the use of resources that reflect a multicultural society adds to the richness of provision for all children and prepares them for their adult lives in a multi-cultural society.

We are part of a world where there are many different languages, accents and dialects. If children are only aware of their own language and ignorant of the existence of others, their experience is very limited. By promoting a positive atmosphere that celebrates language diversity we can enrich the experience of all children, while at the same time valuing the experiences of bilingual children.

OPPOSING DISCRIMINATION

The best way to oppose discrimination is to provide an environment that encourages a positive view of the people of the world, celebrates difference and actively opposes any discriminatory practice.

Opposing discrimination involves developing an understanding of the different practices that may lead to it. This includes being aware of vocabulary or jokes that are, or might be, abusive, and being sensitive and alert to unequal provision of resources and opportunities. Through this knowledge and awareness, child care workers can learn to take positive action and promote equality of opportunity.

Any obvious abuse or discrimination should be challenged. Not to do so would be to accept and condone it. Challenging abuse can be a difficult thing to do, especially for a young worker. It is however a skill that needs to be learned. The ability to deal with discriminatory practices may not be very well developed especially at the beginning of a career. Child care workers should not feel they have failed if they have to take advice about what to do.

If you witness overt discrimination involving adults or children, it may be sufficient initially to make your views known in a calm manner to the people involved. You could then seek advice about alternative strategies and future contact.

Supervisors should be able to give advice and support about the need for further action or what to do if the situation arises again. It may be their duty to take the matter further. Many establishments have an Equal Opportunities Policy or Code of Practice setting out the steps that should be taken.

CREATING A POSITIVE ENVIRONMENT

A positive working environment is achieved primarily through the attitudes and behaviour of all members of the establishment. It can be enhanced by the provision of equipment and activities that avoid cultural and gender bias and present positive images of all children, including those with disabilities. Such provision should permeate both the care and the curriculum that children receive. Providing for good practice should include the following:

- Books, displays and pictorial resources should reflect a multicultural, multi-ability society.
- Resources for practical activities including painting should enable all children to participate fully and represent themselves and their culture.
- The environment and activities should be adapted to enable children with individual and special needs to participate to their full ability.
- Boys and girls should be encouraged to participate in a full range of activities, and to be expressive, active, sensitive and responsive as is appropriate to any situation and not according to gender.
- Plans and provision should be sensitive to parents' different financial circumstances and no child should be excluded because of their parents' means.
- Celebrations and festivities should reflect a multicultural society.
- Wherever possible, carers should be drawn from a variety of backgrounds and include workers of different genders, race and physical abilities. This will encourage understanding, make a clear statement, and enable different children to identify with them.

NOW ANSWER THESE QUESTIONS

1 What factors determine our view of what is 'normal'?
2 In what ways do families differ?
3 What should child care workers do if they witness discrimination?
4 What is the most important factor in providing an anti-discriminatory environment?
5 What resources can be provided for good practice in a child care establishment?

Theories and Development: 0-2 Years

When working with children it is helpful to have an understanding of the principles and theories of child development. Theories concern whether the greatest influence on development is nature, nurture, or the degree to which the child's essential needs are met. By the age of two, an infant will have developed a range of emotional and social skills.

PRINCIPLES OF DEVELOPMENT

Development is an integrated process in which all areas interact with each other. Their interaction results in an individual pattern of development that varies from one child to another. Development is usually made up of a period of rapid growth followed by a period of calm. Children do not develop in isolation; they develop in family systems within a larger cultural system. Social and emotional development includes children's feelings about, and relationships with, other people; their view of themselves; and the development of skills that lead to independence.

Theories of emotional and social development

Theories (ideas) about how and why children develop emotionally and socially are important because they can guide adults to encourage healthy development. There are three main types of theories: biological, learning and psychoanalytical.

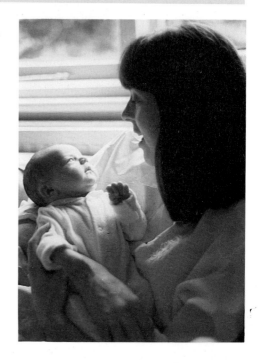

Psychoanalytical theories explain that children only develop healthily if their needs are met

1   Biological theories (the 'nature/heredity' argument) are based on the view that we are born with a genetic make-up that determines how we respond and behave. Our temperament, sociability, emotional responses and intelligence are determined by what we inherit from our biological parents, and our developmental path is programmed in our genes. Biological theories emphasise the role that nature plays in making each child unique and individual. However, taken to extremes, such theories would suggest that adults could have little influence on children's development.

2   Learning theories (the 'nurture/ environment' argument) are based on the belief that children develop by learning from contact with other people, from experiences of reward and punishment and by copying and pretending. These theories emphasise the vital importance of the adult to the developmental process.

3   Psychoanalytical theories are a mixture of biological and learning theories. They argue that children are born with a set of needs (e.g. for love, affection, security and dependence), that these needs are apparent at different stages and that children only develop healthily if they are met.

None of these theories alone gives an adequate explanation of development, but a combination of them is useful in guiding practice with children.

At 12 months, babies:

- Like to be within sight and hearing of a familiar adult; can distinguish between different members of the family and act socially with them; know their own name; will wave goodbye; may be shy with strangers; are capable of a variety of emotional responses including fear, anger happiness and humour; are increasingly aware of the emotions of others.
- Assist with feeding by holding a spoon and may drink from a cup by themselves; help with dressing by holding out their arms or legs.

At 15 months children engage in solitary play.

At 12 months, infants like to be within sight and hearing of a familiar adult and will wave goodbye.

At 18 months children:

- Are still very dependent on a familiar carer; often revert to a fear of strangers; are trying to establish themselves as members of the social group and beginning to internalise the values of people around them; tend to follow their carer around, be sociable and imitate them by helping with small household tasks; are conscious of their family group; imitate and mimic others during their play; engage in solitary or parallel play but like to stay close to a familiar adult or sibling; show some social emotions, e.g. sympathy for someone who is hurt; have intense mood swings.
- Use a cup and spoon well and successfully get food into their mouth; can take off an item of clothing and help with dressing; are still in nappies but can make their carers aware of their toileting needs through words or by restless behaviour.

At 15 months, toddlers:

- Use their main carer as a safe base from which to explore the world; are anxious and apprehensive about physical separation; have an interest in strangers but are either fearful or very wary of them; show interest in other children, but engage only in solitary play; show jealousy of the attention given by adults to other children; are emotionally very unstable, swinging from dependence to independence; resist changes in routine or sudden transitions.
- Hold a cup and drink without assistance; hold a spoon and bring it to the mouth, spilling some food in the process; help with dressing and undressing.

At 18 months toddlers tend to follow their carer around.

NOW ANSWER THESE QUESTIONS

1   What is the relationship of the different developmental areas to one another?
2   What are the three main theories that explain why children develop emotionally and socially?
3   What do each of the theories say about child development?
4   Why is it useful for a child care worker to understand the different theories?
5   What are the emotional and social needs of young children?

Development 2–7 years

Development follows a path that moves from complete immaturity and dependence towards social and emotional maturity and the development of social skills and independence. During the first year, babies who are cared for by a small group of affectionate carers will develop a strong attachment to them and their reactions to other people from 1–3 years will reflect their preference to be with them. From 3 years, they are able to be separated from them happily for increasing periods of time and become increasingly independent of them.

From 3–4 years, children can feel secure when in a strange place away from their main carers

SOCIAL AND EMOTIONAL DEVELOPMENT: 2–4 YEARS

At 2 years, children:

- Do not fully accept that their parent is a separate individual; can sometimes be very self-contained, at other times very dependent; are capable of a wide range of feelings, moods and behavioural changes; are able to empathise with the feelings of those close to them, e.g. if their carer is upset, they are capable of trying to comfort them; are developing new skills with language, enabling them to achieve new levels of social contact; demand their carer's attention and want their needs to be met immediately; will ask for food; can respond to a reasonable request to wait for attention or for the satisfaction of their needs; are loving and responsive; will try to be independent.

- Can point to parts of the body and other features when asked; feed themselves without spilling; raise a cup and put it down; can put on some clothes with supervision; can say when they need the toilet; become dry in the daytime.

At 2 years 6 months, children:

- Are still emotionally and socially very dependent on familiar adult carers; are also capable of being very independent in some of their behaviour; exhibit extremes of mood and behaviour ranging from aggression and withdrawal, awkwardness and helpfulness; are beginning to develop their self-identity; know their name, their position in the family and their gender; play with other children; develop a concept of gender roles.

- Are able to avoid hazards like stairs and hot stoves; are able to use a spoon well and possibly a fork or chopsticks; can get themselves a drink; are able to pour from one container to another; can dress with supervision; unzip zips; unbuckle and buckle and unbutton and button clothing; are toilet-trained during the day and can be dry at night, especially if lifted.

From 3–4 years, children:

- Are usually happier, more contented, friendly and helpful in their manner to others; have gained some physical and emotional control; have more settled feelings and are better able to express them; can feel secure when in a strange place away from their main carers but with familiar people; can show affection for younger siblings; may have imaginary fears and anxieties; show some insecurity, expressed as shyness, irritability and self-consciousness.
- Can use a fork and spoon, chopsticks or hands to eat; can toilet themselves during the day and may be dry through the night; will wash their hands but may have difficulty drying them; are learning to dress without supervision.

SOCIAL AND EMOTIONAL DEVELOPMENT: 4–7 YEARS

At 4 years, children:

- Are constantly trying to understand and make sense of their experiences; can be very sociable but stubborn, using some physical as well as verbal aggression; may have one particular friend; are confident and assured, but may be afraid of the dark and have other fears; turn to adults for comfort.
- Can feed themselves proficiently; are able to dress and undress themselves, but may have difficulty with back buttons, ties and laces; can wash and dry hands and face and clean teeth.

At 5 years, children:

- Are achieving a level of balance, self-containment and independence; are usually friendly, willing to talk to anyone and able to be polite; want the approval of adults; enjoy brief separations from home and carers; show good control of emotions; are increasingly aware of differences between themselves and other people, including gender and status; are developing a sense of shame.
- Can use a knife and fork well; are able to dress and undress; may be able to lace shoes and tie ties; can wash and dry face and hands, but need supervision to complete other washing.

From 6–7 years children:

- Are progressing a long way along the path to independence and maturity; are developing a wide range of appropriate emotional responses; are able to behave appropriately in a variety of social situations; are growing steadily more independent and truly sociable, are generally self-confident and friendly; are able to co-operate in quite sophisticated ways with adults and children.
- Are finishing learning all the basic skills needed for independence in eating, hygiene and toileting.

NOW ANSWER THESE QUESTIONS

1. Describe the path that children follow in their emotional and social development.
2. What are some key aspects of a 2-year-old's behaviour?
3. How do children of 3–4 years generally behave to other people?
4. What have children generally achieved by 5 years ?
5. What are the basic skills of a child of 7 years?

Separation and Transitions

In order for healthy emotional and social development to take place, children's need of love, stability and security must be met. The movement of a child from one place of care to another is known as **transition**. Transitions should be handled sensitively so that a child's sense of trust is not damaged. Preparation and good care will help a child to cope with separation.

THE NEEDS OF CHILDREN

Children have basic needs that must be met for their healthy emotional and social growth and development. They need:

- **Love and affection.** This means unconditional love – knowing that whatever they do, they will always be loved by their closest carers. They must experience a close bond of attachment with at least one adult carer, preferably built up during the first year and at least by the time they are three years old.
- **Stability and security** in their environment. This can be found in a stable family, where relationships are positive, where they are cared for consistently by a small group of familiar carers, and where there are established routines and reasonable guidelines for their behaviour.
- **Praise and encouragement.** This will make them feel valued and worthwhile.
- **Appropriate responsibility**. This enables children to gain personal independence and become confident and able to accept responsibility as they mature.

Some children experience frequent moves caused by constant and unpredictable family breakdowns

TRANSITIONS AND THE EXPERIENCE OF SEPARATION AND LOSS

Transitions are the movement of a child from one place of care to another. They usually involve separation from the main carer and a change of physical environment. They can cause a child to feel a sense of loss.

The loss of a main carer for even a short period can adversely affect a child's sense of stability, security and trust. In general, children react most strongly to separation between the ages of six months and three years.

Periods of transition

- Some children have to adapt to transitions when they are very young and are placed in day care. This is the period when they have developed a strong attachment to their parent, but have not become independent enough to cope without help. Good substitute care is essential.
- Children may experience loss, anxiety and stress when they start school. Effective school admission policies are needed.
- Some children may experience total loss when a parent leaves home, goes to prison, or dies, or if for any reason the child is placed in full time care. The child will need considerable support and understanding to help them deal with feelings including grief, uncertainty and guilt.

Children are immature and vulnerable. They need special help and care to cope with transition and change. Preparation aids children's reactions to transitions and has become part of the policy of most nurseries, schools, hospitals, childminders, and long-term foster care agencies.

Before a transition, child care workers should prepare children by:

- Being sensitive to their needs and stage of development
- Talking, listening, explaining and reassuring them honestly about what will happen
- Reading books and watching relevant videos with them
- Providing experiences of imaginative and expressive play that help them to express their feelings
- Arranging introductory visits for them and their carers
- Ensuring that any relevant details about them, including their cultural background, are available to the substitute carer

Caring for children

During a transition, the care provided for children should take into account the following:

- The younger the child, the more they benefit from a one-to-one relationship with a specific person. This is especially true for children under three years.
- The particular needs and background of each child need to be known.
- Children's comfort objects should be readily available to them.
- Children should be provided with appropriate activities, including play that encourages the expression of feelings. In the long term, unresolved feelings can return to complicate adult mental health.
- Nursery and school policies can help if they include an appropriate admission programme, stagger the intake of children, have an informative brochure in the parents' home language,+ good liaison with parents, and a welcoming environment.

Reuniting the child with parents

There are several factors that help in the process of reuniting children with parents:

- The child's parent/carers should have access to them whenever possible and appropriate.
- Honest reassurance should be given about the length of the separation.
- Positive reminders of parent/carers should be promoted at all times.
- Parent/carers should be warned to expect some difficult or regressive behaviour. This is the child expressing anger and sadness at being separated.

FREQUENT AND MULTIPLE TRANSITIONS.

Children whose admission to school is handled sensitively usually learn to cope with attending school each day. Children can also be helped to adjust to frequent hospital admissions or regular respite foster care.

Some children however, experience frequent moves. This may be caused by constant and unpredictable family breakdowns.

Such children become increasingly mistrustful of adults. They become accustomed to change, but become increasingly unable to relate closely to any carers. Their emotional and social development is disturbed and this makes them difficult to care for. For this reason frequent changes of environment for young children should be avoided if at all possible.

NOW ANSWER THESE QUESTIONS

1 What are the emotional needs of children?
2 What is a transition?
3 Why can transitions be difficult for children?
4 What is the best way to help a child cope with separation?
5 Why can frequent changes be damaging for a child?

36 Encouraging Children's Development

Adults should encourage children to develop a good self-image, high self-esteem, and independence and self-help skills appropriate to their developmental level. Children may need help in learning to relate to others. Sometimes they can experience strong feelings, especially if they lose someone they are attached to. An adult can help children to deal with strong feelings of loss and grief.

SELF-IMAGE AND IDENTITY

A child's self-image and identity is their view of who they are and what they are like. Children who have a positive self-image think well of themselves and are more positive about life.

Those with high self-esteem form and maintain good relationships with others; are more likely to feel valued, to be independent, self-reliant, to achieve more in life and to be happy. Encouraging children to develop high self-esteem is therefore very important.

Childcare and education workers should understand the importance of high self-esteem and how to encourage it. The experience of good early relationships is of great significance and workers can help by forming good, caring relationships with children.

Encouraging self-esteem

The responses of adults are very important to the child's self-concept. Adults should value what children do and praise their efforts and achievements whenever possible.
Every child should see positive images of themselves and their social and cultural background reflected in the visual images that surround them.

Children's behaviour may be challenged but they should never be 'put down' or made to feel bad. Children need to be given clear guidelines and boundaries for acceptable behaviour and these should be consistently applied.

Helping children to achieve self-help skills

As children develop, they need to be encouraged to achieve new self-help skills and praised when they do so.

● Tasks should be manageable and appro-priate to their age and stage of development so that they can experience a sense of achievement, not failure.

Tasks should be manageable and appro-priate to children's age and stage of development so that they can have a sense of achievement

● Children respond well to having things set apart as their own; this makes them feel independent, important and valued.
● Avoid gender stereotyping and other forms of labelling. This can have a profound effect on a child's aspirations and achievements.

Helping children to relate to others

Adults need to provide suitable play and experiences to help children relate to each other. This requires a sound knowledge of children's developing ability to recognise the feelings of others.

Up to the age of two, children are unable to take others' feelings into account and play is solitary. Between two and three, they begin to understand that others have feelings, and to watch and play alongside them (**parallel play**). Between three and four years, children are more conscious of others and will begin to join in with their play.

From four years, children have developed a stable self-concept and are able to play with others, although conflicts are inevitable and they may need help to deal with them.

Child care workers can provide activities that encourage co-operation, taking turns, sharing and working together. They need to judge when it is appropriate to intervene in conflicts (if children do not have the skills to deal with them themselves, or are in danger); and when it is better to leave them to deal with conflicts themselves so that they have a chance to learn how to resolve problems themselves.

Hurtful behaviour must be challenged and discussed with all involved so that children can deal with situations better in the future.

DEALING WITH LOSS AND GRIEF

Grief is the feeling of deep sorrow at the death of a loved person. Children can also experience loss when parents separate, are hospitalised, go to prison or move abroad, or when they are separated from anybody to whom they have formed a close attachment. Grief follows a recognisable path or pattern. Child care and education workers need to understand the child's feelings and behaviour and help them to understand that their reactions are normal.

STAGE OF GRIEF	CHILD'S REACTION
Early grief	Immediately after the death or loss, a child may feel shock, numbness, disbelief, denial, panic, alarm, and may be lifeless, or hyperactive, dislike being alone, and be prone to illness.
Acute grief	Following the acceptance of the loss, a child may feel extreme sadness, anger, guilt, shame, yearning, and despair. They may pine, search, be restless, cry, carry out compulsive irrational acts, lack concentration, be prone to illness.
Subsiding grief	Acute feelings have now been worked through and a child may be less absorbed by grief, have better concentration, be calmer, less preoccupied, show interest in other things, demonstrate higher self-esteem, form other attachments and become involved in other activities.

PROVIDING FOR A GRIEVING CHILD

Grief can be a very powerful experience. The growth of a child may be affected in every area and care must be taken to safeguard their all-round development.

Child care workers can be of great help to a child at this time. They can give the child uncomplicated attention and consideration. They need to be honest, provide physical comfort and a quiet environment; to listen and allow the child to express feelings; to give the child time and attention; to help them to be patient with their feelings; to reassure them; to make allowances for regression, restless behaviour and lack of concentration; to provide opportunities for expressive play; to make few demands; to help the child to organise themselves; to protect them and share their feelings, and help them focus on the future.

Different cultures have different practices for dealing with grief and mourning. It is important to have a knowledge of and respect for different customs and beliefs.

NOW ANSWER THESE QUESTIONS

1 Why is a positive self-image and high self-esteem important to a child's development?
2 How can children be encouraged to develop new self-help skills?
3 What can be done to help children to relate to others?
4 What are the main stages of grief?
5 How can children be helped to cope with loss?

37

Understanding and Assessing Behaviour

To understand children's behaviour it is important to know what behaviour is and how it is acquired. The development of children's behaviour follows an observable path and pattern. It is possible to describe normal behavioural characteristics at different ages and stages of development. Behaviour is affected by how a child's needs are met and by prior events known as **antecedents**. Partnership with parents is essential when caring for children.

Carers need a thorough understanding of the behaviour that is normal and to be expected at specific ages

DEFINING BEHAVIOUR

By 'behaviour', we mean:

- Almost all the things we do and say
- The way we act and react to other people and our environment.
- Both the acceptable and unacceptable things we do

Behaviour is acquired through learning in different ways, but mainly by:

- Becoming aware of the expectations of family and close carers
- Being immersed in the customs of a social and cultural group
- Copying and imitating other people, especially through play
- Being given rewards and sanctions
- Identifying with a peer group

UNDERSTANDING AND ASSESSING BEHAVIOUR

Carers need a thorough understanding of the behaviour that is 'normal' and to be expected at specific ages. Children learn patterns of behaviour; these patterns change as they grow and mature. Throughout childhood, children develop:

- An increasing range of emotions and behaviour appropriate to a wide range of situations
- A greater degree of independence and control over their feelings and behaviour
- A deeper understanding and acceptance of the feelings and behaviour of others and less need for external constraints on their behaviour, i.e. discipline

When assessing a child's behaviour, carers need to consider whether it is 'age-appropriate'. Understanding what is and is not age-appro-

priate will enable them to have realistic expectations; to set boundaries that the child can stay within, to assess the behaviour and respond appropriately. It will also help them to avoid punishing the child for what is in fact 'normal' behaviour for that age.

Children's needs

Children have many emotional and social needs. When trying to understand and assess a child's behaviour, it is important to consider the extent to which those needs are being met. All children need affection, a sense of belonging, to be handled consistently, to have a growing sense of independence and achievement, to develop high self-esteem and to feel the approval of others. In the child's family environment, for a wide variety of reasons, these needs may or may not be met.

CHANGES IN CHILDREN'S BEHAVIOUR

Changes in children's behaviour will occur naturally as part of the normal developmental maturing process. But sudden changes in behaviour are more likely to have a specific cause. When trying to understand and assess children's behaviour it is important to try to find out the cause – including whether the child fully understands the rules for acceptable behaviour in that setting. The **antecedents** (what happened before the behaviour occurred, either recently or in the past) are also often of great importance.

An antecedent to a particular type of behaviour may be the experience of some kind of stress. This may include:

- Change of carer, routine, home, school or family structure
- Stress caused by the birth of a sibling or separation of parents
- Loss of any kind (e.g. of a significant person through death or separation) or of a loved object

Understanding antecedents is an important aspect of managing children's behaviour successfully. Without it a child may simply be labelled as being 'difficult' or 'naughty'. This stereotyping is not only a negative experience for the child, but fails to provide a framework for managing their behaviour. The usual result is that the behaviour simply becomes more extreme.

The arrival of a baby brother or sister can give rise to sibling jealousy

WORKING WITH PARENTS

When managing children's behaviour it is essential for child care and education workers to work in partnership with parents and other professionals.

Workers have two responsibilities:

1 To adhere to the policies of the organisation in which they work

2 To respect the wishes of parents

Sometimes it may be difficult to do both. Careful consideration should be given to how to meet both responsibilities.

NOW ANSWER THESE QUESTIONS

1 How do children learn behaviour?
2 What do children gain greater control over as they grow and mature?
3 What does 'age-appropriate' behaviour mean?
4 Name three emotional needs of a child.
5 What is an 'antecedent' to behaviour?

38 Ages and Stages of Development

Children's behaviour follows a recognisable path and pattern. Because of this, it is possible to say that certain behaviour is typical of a child at a certain age. At the age of one, children's behaviour is characterised by a lack of self-awareness or self-control; by the age of seven, they are capable of a wide range of appropriate emotional and behavioural responses to a range of different situations.

STAGES OF DEVELOPMENT: 1–4 YEARS

At one year, children:

- Do not have a clear perception of themselves as individuals; have a close attachment to, and are sociable with, adults they know; are anxious if separated from them and shy with strangers; are capable of varied emotional responses including rage when thwarted; seek attention vocally and obey simple verbal instructions.

At 15 months, children:

- Are more aware of themselves as individuals, but less of other people as separate from them; explore their environment indiscriminately (they are 'into everything'); are possessive of people they are attached to, and of objects they want ("It's *mine*!"); respond better to distraction than verbal reasoning or sharp discipline; may show off, throw toys in anger, and have mood swings.

At 18 months, children:

- Respond to the word 'No', but usually need the command to be reinforced or repeated; become more aware of themselves as separate individuals; are very self-centred (egocentric) in their awareness and behaviour, having only recently discovered themselves as separate individuals; are very curious about everything around them; cannot tolerate frustration; can be defiant and resistant to adults in an effort to protect themselves and their individuality.

At two years, children:

- Have a clear understanding of self but are still not fully aware of carers as separate

By the age of four, children engage in elaborate and prolonged imaginative play

individuals; are able to be self-contained for periods of time; are often possessive of toys and have little idea of sharing; want their demands to be met quickly but can wait if asked; may have tantrums if crossed or frustrated but can be distracted; have a wide range of feelings and are capable of loving, responsive behaviour; are aware of and able to respond to the feelings of others.

By the age of three, children:

- Develop a strong self-identity and a growing level of independence; show less anxiety about separation and strangers; often resist efforts by carers to limit their behaviour; have mood swings and extremes of behaviour; are impulsive, less easily distracted; can wait for their needs to be met; are less rebellious and use language rather than physical outbursts to express themselves; are ready to respond to reasoning and bargaining; are beginning to learn the appropriate behaviour for a range of different social settings; can understand when it is necessary to be quiet or noisy; adopt the attitudes and moods of adults; want the approval of loved adults.

By the age of four, children:

● Gain more physical and emotional self-control; have more settled feelings and are more balanced in their expression of them; are more independent of their main carers; are happier, more friendly and helpful; can respond to reason and bargaining as well as to distraction; are less rebellious and can learn the appropriate behaviour for a range of settings; are capable of playing with groups of children, tending to centre around an activity then dissolve and reform; can take turns but are not consistent about this; are often very dramatic in their play; engage in elaborate and prolonged imaginative play; are developing a strong sense of past and future; can be dogmatic and argumentative; may blame others when they misbehave; may even behave badly in order to get a reaction; may swear and use bad language.

STAGES OF DEVELOPMENT: 4–7 YEARS

Between 4 and 5 years, children:

● Are constantly trying to make sense of the world around them and their experiences in it; can be very sociable, talkative, confident, purposeful, persistent and self-assured; can take turns and wait for their needs to be met; may also be stubborn and sometimes aggressive and argumentative; still turn to adults for comfort especially when tired, ill or hurt.

At five years, children:

● Have achieved a greater level of independence and self-containment; generally show a well-developed level of control over their emotions; show a desire to do well and to gain the approval of adults; are developing a sense of shame if their behaviour is unacceptable to the adult; can also be argumentative, show off, boast and be over-active at times of conflict; argue with parents when they request something; still respond to discipline based on bargaining; are not so easily distracted from their own anger as when they were younger; may regain their balance by having 'time-out'; prefer games of rivalry to team games; enjoy co-operative group play, but often need an adult to arbitrate; boast, show off and threaten; show a desire to excel and can be purposeful and persistent.

Between 6 and 7 years, children:

● Become increasingly mature and independent; develop a wide range of appropriate emotional and behavioural responses to different situations; are able to behave appropriately in a variety of social situations; can be self-confident, friendly and co-operative; may have spells of being irritable, rebellious and sulky.

NOW ANSWER THESE QUESTIONS

1 What is the usual behaviour of a one-year-old towards strangers?
2 What is the typical response of a two-year-old to being thwarted?
3 What can a four-year-old respond to in addition to distraction?
4 What does a typical five-year-old want to gain from adults?
5 What have children achieved by the time they are seven?

39

A Framework for Children's Behaviour

Normal behaviour is the behaviour to be expected at a specific age. A framework for children's behaviour provides an agreed approach to how children should be encouraged to behave within a child care setting. It involves goals and boundaries based on values. These define what is considered to be 'acceptable behaviour'.

'NORMAL' BEHAVIOUR

The concept of behaviour being 'normal' at a certain age is a useful broad tool to use when observing and assessing children's behaviour. Having an awareness of what to expect also helps us to manage children's behaviour. Parents and carers sometimes show a lack of awareness of what is normal at a particular stage of the developmental process. As a result they have unrealistic expectations of their children, respond negatively to their behaviour and then punish them. If we know that temper tantrums are normal in a child of two years, or that curiosity and the drive to explore are predictable in a very young child, it helps us to respond firmly yet positively.

Normal behaviour is the behaviour to be expected at a specific age. Different children achieve maturity in their behaviour at different ages. The age at which children develop specific behavioural patterns is only approximate and depends on:

Cultural differences can easily be accommodated positively in a child care setting

- The characteristics of the individual child
- The child's family, social and cultural environment and the expectations placed on the child within this environment
- Whether the child has any individual special needs – for example, a physical or learning impairment.

GOALS AND BOUNDARIES

Most children will develop 'normal' and acceptable, patterns of behaviour if adults are consistent, loving and fair in their expectations, are good role models, and if they set a clear **framework** for behaviour. A framework is made up of a set of goals and boundaries:

- **Goals** are the behaviour that adults want to encourage, and should cover all aspects of behaviour within the setting, including social, physical and verbal. They cover how children and adults should behave towards one another, including sharing, taking turns, being courteous and helping others when they are distressed. Expectations of children's behaviour must be realistic and achievable in relation to the children's age and stage of development, and must be understandable to all.

- **Boundaries** are the limits of what is considered acceptable behaviour. Children need to know that if they cross the boundary of acceptable behaviour they will be sanctioned. Boundaries are usually set to exclude physical aggression, verbal abuse, and throwing or destroying equipment.

VALUES AND NORMS

A framework for children's behaviour should be based on a set of values and norms that can be understood by all.

The behaviour children learn at home is based on the values and norms of the social and cultural group to which they belong.

- A **value** is something that is believed to be important and worthwhile, e.g. that everyone is worthy of care and attention. Norms are rules or customs of actual behaviour that are based on values and beliefs.
- A **norm** is that children should listen if their teacher is talking to them - the norm being based on a belief in the value of learning.

Many social and cultural groups share similar values and beliefs about what is acceptable or unacceptable behaviour, e.g. the belief that physical violence is wrong and that respect for other people is important.

Sometimes groups of people have differing values or beliefs, together with different rules and customs. For example, groups have different rules and customs about how to address and relate to other people; what is appropriate dress; how food should be eaten etc. These differences may mean that parents and schools have different expectations of their children's behaviour. However such differences need not be negative and many can easily be accommodated positively within a child care setting.

If they conflict with the values and norms of the setting, workers and parents must develop a clear understanding of what is acceptable within the child care establishment. For example, there could be different beliefs about the value of punishment and how it should be carried out.

Child care and education workers also have their own personal set of values about acceptable or unacceptable behaviour. These are not necessarily the values that are appropriate to a child care setting. It is essential that workers develop a professional approach when working with children and adopt the values of the setting.

Accepting the child

It is not useful to describe a child as 'naughty' or 'bad'. This can have a negative effect on a child's self-esteem and feelings of worth, and lead to the child feeling rejected and unwanted. Criticism should focus on the behaviour, not the child. Behaviour is most usefully described as 'acceptable' or 'unacceptable', according to the social context in which it occurs.

NOW ANSWER THESE QUESTIONS

1 What is normal behaviour?
2 What are goals and boundaries?
3 What is the difference between a value and a norm?
4 Give an example of a commonly shared norm of children's behaviour in a school.
5 Why is it not useful to describe a child as 'naughty'?

40 Managing Children's Behaviour

Behaviour modification is a useful tool for child care and education workers to use when managing children's behaviour. It involves identifying positive aspects of behaviour and encouraging them through praise and recognition. Unwanted behaviour can be discouraged by ignoring it or through the use of sanctions. Management of persistent problem behaviour requires a team approach to adopt appropriate policies and responses.

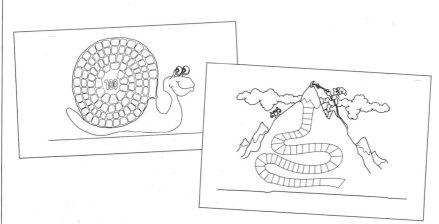

Merit charts displayed on walls around the setting can encourage positive behaviour

WHAT IS BEHAVIOUR MODIFICATION?

Behaviour modification is the name given to techniques used to influence children's behaviour. It works by:

- Promoting and rewarding positive aspects of children's behaviour
- Managing and discouraging negative aspects of children's behaviour

It is a useful tool for child care and education workers to use when managing children's behaviour.

Behaviour modification involves:

1   Identifying behaviour
The first aim of behaviour modification is to identify different types of behaviour. These are both the behaviour that the adult wishes to encourage, including:

- Playing co-operatively and sharing toys
- Being considerate and helpful
- Working well and completing a task

– and the behaviour that the adult wishes to discourage, including:

- Aggressive, abusive or challenging behaviour
- Behaviour that is disruptive, destructive or damaging to people or property
- Self-damaging or personally unconstructive behaviour

2   Rewarding positive behaviour
The second aim is to reward positive behaviour by encouraging and promoting it.
This may involve giving a child:

- Positive attention through words of praise or encouragement or non-verbal attention such as smiles, nods or hugs
- Practical treats such as sweets, stickers, badges or toys
- The opportunity to share rewards. This might be done by, for example, recording each child's positive behaviour on a chart (see illustration above), so that the 'points' gradually accumulate and the whole group gets a reward when the chart is full

40

3 Discouraging negative behaviour

The third aim is to discourage negative behaviour. This may involve:

- Ignoring the behaviour
- Directing attention to another child who is behaving acceptably
- Removing the child to a different, unrewarding situation
- Showing disapproval verbally or non-verbally
- Applying the sanctions agreed by the establishment, e.g. loss of privileges
- Using physical restraint if it is in the interests of the safety of the child or others

Note that physical punishment is illegal and should never be used in a child care establishment.

Behaviour modification techniques can be very effective, but they need to be used consistently by all the adults concerned with the child. This can be difficult to achieve and requires both a team approach and partnership between child care workers and parents. Adults need to have a clear idea of the behaviour they are trying to modify and then observe, record and assess changes in behaviour in order to monitor the effectiveness of their approach.

MANAGING PROBLEM BEHAVIOUR

Management of persistent problem behaviour presents a challenge to child care workers. A clear policy and a team approach are needed.

Behaviour which is directly challenging should be responded to calmly, using the techniques described above. Challenging behaviour is usually attention-seeking and may be self-destructive. It is often the result of a child only being given attention when they misbehave. An effective method of changing such behaviour is consistently to give the child lots of positive attention and to praise them when they behave acceptably. Attention-seeking behaviour should then be ignored, provided it is not too destructive or placing anyone in danger. The child then learns to associate attention with acceptable rather than unacceptable behaviour.

Reporting to parents

Persistent unwanted behaviour should be reported to parents promptly and accurately in recognition of their rights and responsibilities, and to ensure partnership with parents.

It is important to share issues with colleagues and discuss the management of children's behaviour with them. The benefit of a team approach is that it provides support for colleagues and consistency in dealing with a particular child or group.

Physical punishment

Appropriate policies and responses should be discussed and agreed so that everyone is working to the same goals. The use of physical punishment is not allowed in child care establishments. Physical restraint to prevent injury or damage must be very carefully administered. Consideration should be given to whether it is appropriate to seek specialist help and guidance from educational or child psychologists or psychiatrists.

Significant incidents should be recorded accurately and objectively. This means only recording what actually took place, not the reactions or opinions of workers. Such records can then be referred to by other colleagues and if necessary used as evidence.

NOW ANSWER THESE QUESTIONS

1 What is behaviour modification?
2 What are the first two steps of behaviour modification?
3 How can an adult encourage acceptable behaviour?
4 What is an effective way of discouraging unwanted behaviour?
5 What steps might need to be taken if problem behaviour persists?

41

Partnership with Parents and Carers

Everyone who works with children needs to recognise the importance of establishing a good relationship with the child's parents or main carer. The basis of this relationship should be a desire to work in co-operation in the interests of the child. To do this successfully you need to understand how such relationships are established.

Child care workers must recognise the value of parental involvement and understand how it can support their work with children.

ROLE OF PARENTS AND CARERS

To work successfully with children and their parents, it is essential for child care workers to understand the central role that parents have in their children's lives, and the role they have in the partnership with the child care setting. It is important for the child care worker to acknowledge that:

- Parents are the main carers and educators of their children.

- Parents know and understand their children and can share this knowledge with the staff to the benefit of the children.
- Parents are partners with child care workers in the care and education of their children.
- Parents have skills and experience that can be of value to the child care setting.
- Parents will value being involved in the care and education of their children.

WORKING WITH PARENTS

Parents can be involved in a child care setting in many different ways. With the right support and encouragement from the staff, each will develop the role they prefer. Parents may:

- Work with the children, involving themselves in activities, helping with reading, swimming and outings
- Help with parties, fairs, concerts etc.
- Support children at home, by listening to them read or helping with other work
- Form support groups for themselves or the setting, e.g. a home-school association
- Become involved as a governor or committee member

Parents can be involved in a child care setting

ROLE OF THE CHILD CARE WORKER

Sharing the care and management of children effectively with parents will provide continuity between the family and the care and education setting. The child care worker should:

- Respect the parents' values, practices and expressed wishes
- Exchange ideas, views and plans with parents

- Provide continuity and consistency
- Offer reassurance and encouragement to parents and get advice from other sources if necessary
- Emphasise the central role of parents in the children's lives
- Reinforce the confidence of parents in their role
- Establish procedures for emergencies

RESPONDING TO PARENTS IN DIFFICULT SITUATIONS

In some situations parents may react in a way which brings them into conflict with members of staff. This can be for a number of reasons:

- They may be experiencing stress in their own lives, perhaps because of unsatisfactory living conditions or personal problems
- They may lack confidence in their child-rearing abilities
- They may have legitimate complaints and concerns about a staff member
- They may disagree with the methods used in the setting or be worried about their child's progress/behaviour

- They may not be keeping to their commitments: for example, not arriving on time to collect their children

It is important for child care workers to recognise and deal with any such situations as effectively as they can. You should always:

- Take any expressed concern seriously
- Stay calm and be courteous
- Acknowledge the parent's feelings and opinions
- Be non-judgemental
- Be supportive to parents
- Challenge your own prejudices

SETTLING CHILDREN INTO THE CHILD CARE SETTING

Parents should stay if possible while the child becomes familiar with the child care environment

Settling in should be a planned process. It is important to settle a child gradually, with the child and the parent separating in stages. The time taken to settle a child will depend mainly on the child's age and their previous experience of separation from the parent. Parents need to be clear about, and agree to,

the settling-in arrangements. The needs of children and parents should be taken into account. You should explain to them about:

- The setting
- The staff and other adult helpers
- Play and activities
- Food and how preferences are catered for
- Arrangements for emergencies
- Hours of operation
- Fees (if appropriate)
- Policies on confidentiality
- Any items they are expected to provide

If possible, parents should be encouraged to stay while the child becomes familiar with the new environment. Gradually they should leave them for longer periods each day, leaving the child with something familiar such as a favourite toy to bridge the period of separation. A policy of open communication should be encouraged so that any problems can be dealt with at an early stage.

NOW ANSWER THESE QUESTIONS

1. Who are the main carers and educators of children?
2. Explain the role of the child care worker in the partnership with parents.
3. What important points must be considered when settling a child into a new setting?
4. List four ways that parents might involve themselves in the setting.
5. Summarise the preferred actions of a child care worker in a situation of conflict with a parent.

42 Communicating with Parents

When communicating with parents, child care workers should make it clear that they are welcome in the setting. Communication should be a two-way process and should benefit the worker, the parents and the child. The way you communicate with parents should promote confidence in the service provided.

PROMOTING COMMUNICATION

*To ensure good communication with parents,
child care workers should:*

Maintain confidentiality

Provide information

Make time for parents
to talk to you

Make the
environment friendly
and welcoming

Acknowledge
and address
carers by their
preferred name

Listen to
parents
and respond,
giving them
your full
attention

Organise help if you need
someone to interpret

Be friendly and
approachable

Resolve conflict

Share information

Show understanding

Provide information

42

EXCHANGING INFORMATION

Children will benefit if there is a regular exchange of information between parents and the child care worker.

Parents need to be given information about the setting, including:

- How children will spend the day
- What commitments parents are expected to make (fees, times etc.)
- Safety policies
- Philosophy of the setting
- Curriculum methods

Parents need to have the opportunity to give information to the staff and to discuss their child's progress.

Remember: communication is a two-way process.

Written records

Written records provide essential information about the child, the parents and anyone else who cares for the child. It is important that the information recorded is kept up to date. Records should be stored securely and confidentiality maintained.

Records vary but usually contain:

- Personal details, names, address etc.
- Names, addresses and phone numbers of main carers
- Emergency contact numbers
- Medical details
- Dietary and other needs which may affect the care of the child

Other information may include the name of the child's health visitor and social worker.

WRITTEN COMMUNICATIONS

Parents will receive a range of written communications from the child care establishment. It is important that these are clear, informative and written in a friendly manner.

Most settings will have a brochure that will give information about what is offered. This will probably include:

- Address and telephone number
- Times of opening
- Age range of children cared for
- Admission policy
- Information about fees and meals
- Qualifications of the staff
- Philosophy of the setting
- What parents are expected to provide, and any other commitments, e.g. notice if leaving
- Details of curriculum and methods used

Most child care settings provide a booklet containing basic information for parents and children

NOW ANSWER THESE QUESTIONS

1. Give **four** examples of how you could ensure good communication with parents.
2. How will children benefit from a regular exchange of information between parents and child care workers?
3. What important points do you need to remember about keeping written records?
4. What are the important features of any written communications that parents receive?
5. What information about the children may be held on record?

43 The Legal and Political Framework

A wide range of organisations exist to provide services for young children and their families. Some of these are statutory (i.e. provided directly by the state), others are voluntary (i.e. provided by organisations funded by donations and/or some state funding). Others are private (i.e. provided by businesses to meet a demand and yield a profit for their owners).

STATE PROVISION

Great Britain is a democracy. This means that its citizens have the opportunity, at regular intervals, to vote for the people who govern them (politicians). Government involves politicians being aware of the needs of citizens and deciding whether and how to meet these needs. To do this they pass legislation. For example, in the nineteenth century the government recognised the need of people to have clean water and sanitation and spent government money to provide this.

Politicians hold different views on how far the state should go in providing support for its citizens. This is reflected in the different policies of the main political parties.

Great Britain is a democracy

THE WELFARE STATE

Britain's Welfare State was introduced in the mid-to-late 1940s. It was based on the belief that the government was responsible for its citizens' welfare. The aim was to eliminate poverty and to provide education and health care for all. If you talk to someone who was born before 1930 you will get an interesting picture of life in Britain before the Welfare State. Life was difficult for people if they had no job and no money to pay for medical care.

The Welfare State has been successful in achieving its basic aims through statutory services, e.g. the National Health Service, Education, and Social Security. However, demand for services continues to rise and it has become increasingly expensive to run. Recent governments have encouraged people to be more independent and to pay for services.

STATUTORY SERVICES

The provision of state services for children and their families is complex. A statutory service is one that exists because parliament has passed a law to say that the service either *must* or *can* be provided. Some services are provided by central government departments and funded from central taxation. Others are provided by local government and funded from a combination of local and central taxation. The provision of services is undergoing change as some county councils and district councils are being combined to form unitary authorities.

Statutory service providers
Both central and local government departments provide services for children and their families (see table opposite).

SERVICE/DEPT.	PROVIDER	FUNDING
National Health Service Department of Education (for policy and grant-maintained schools) Department of Social Security	Central government departments, organised into regional offices	Out of central taxation (income tax, VAT, national insurance)
Education Department (for LEA schools) Social Services Department Leisure Services Housing Department	Local government departments (including those of county councils, urban and rural district councils and unitary authorities) organised into local offices	From local taxation (the Community Charge) and from central taxation in the form of grants from central to local government

VOLUNTARY PROVISION

There is a strong tradition of voluntary provision in Britain by organisations such as Barnados, the NCH, SCOPE etc. These organisations are founded by people who see a need and are determined to meet it. Money originally comes from donations, but nowadays some organisations are subsidised by the state.

As well as volunteers, staff are often paid and trained to provide a service in the same way as in state-run organisations. The main difference is that their existence is not determined by government legislation but by individuals. The government has encouraged the growth of this sector in order to reduce the role of the state.

Private provision

Recently there has been an increase in the number of services offered by private providers, e.g. day nurseries, care assistants, health care etc. As with the voluntary sector, these are often very professional services with trained and qualified staff. Staff are paid, but costs are sometimes kept to a minimum because one of the aims of such organisations is to make money

There is a strong tradition of service provision by voluntary organisations in Britain

for their owners. Private providers of childcare must meet the requirements laid down by government, especially The Children Act 1989. Since 1979 governments have encouraged the growth of the private sector. However, not all people can afford to pay for such services. There is now a tendency for those who can to pay, and those who cannot to rely on the state.

Because of under-funding, state provision is not always as good as private, e.g. many state school buildings are in need of repair and hospitals have long waiting lists.

NOW ANSWER THESE QUESTIONS

1 What is a statutory service?
2 What was the original aim of the Welfare State?
3 Why are voluntary organisations formed?
4 What is the main difference between voluntary and statutory organisations?
5 What are two aims of private organisations?

Education and Social Services

The main statutory services for children and their families are provided by the Education Department and the Social Services Department of each local authority. Policies and curriculum are based on laws passed by central government. The Education Reform Act 1988 and The Children Act 1989 are the most important pieces of recent legislation affecting child care in the UK.

PRIMARY EDUCATION AND THE NATIONAL CURRICULUM

The state is required by law to ensure that all children of statutory school age, including those with disabilities, receive education. This must be from the beginning of the term after their fifth birthday until the end of the school year in which they have their sixteenth birthday.

The structure of school provision varies from one local authority area to another. It may consist of one primary school until eleven years, or an infant school followed by a junior school until eleven years, or a first school followed by a middle school.

All state schools are now required by law to follow the **National Curriculum**. The aim is to ensure that all children follow a broad-based and balanced curriculum and study certain core subjects. The content of the National Curriculum and arrangements for testing it have been continuously changed.

Nursery schools and classes

Local authorities have the power (but not a duty) to provide pre-school education. Some choose not to use their powers and as a result the national provision of nursery education varies, with high provision in some areas and none in others. Nursery schools or nursery units attached to

primary schools are often found in areas of highest social deprivation and need. Nursery education is usually part-time, either each morning or afternoon, and there is a strong emphasis on play and exploration. Where there is no nursery provision, some local authorities admit 'rising fives' (children between four and five years) into primary schools. Most European countries have more nursery education than Britain.

Providers of State funded nursery education are required to provide a programme that promotes the **Desirable Outcomes** for Children's learning by the time they are five years old.

The state is required by law to ensure that all children including those with disabilities who are of statutory school age receive education

SCHOOLS AND GRANT-MAINTAINED STATUS

Until the Education Reform Act 1988, all state schools were under the control of their Local Education Authority (LEA). In passing this law the government aimed to encourage schools to

'opt out' of local authority control and have 'grant-maintained status' (GMS). This means that they receive their money (grant) directly from the government, not from their local authority. This money is used by the school in the way they choose, free of any LEA influence, to pay staff and to buy the services they need.

At present only a small proportion of schools have chosen to opt for grant-maintained status. Those that have not 'opted out' now receive a much larger proportion of their education budget directly from the LEA. The head teacher and the governors of each school decide how to spend this money. They are responsible for the financial and overall management of their school. This system is called the **Local Management of Schools (LMS)**.

SOCIAL SERVICES

Local authorities provide personal social services through their **Social Services Departments (SSDs)**. The Children Act 1989 gave them a duty to provide services for children in need in their area, to help them to stay with their families and be brought up by them.

Children are defined by The Children Act 1989 as being 'in need' if:

1 They are unlikely to achieve or maintain, or to have the opportunity of achieving or maintaining, a reasonable standard of health or development without the provision of services
2 Their health or development is likely to be significantly impaired, or further impaired, without the provision of such services
3 They are disabled

The SSD tries to keep families together by:

● Offering them support in the community and through family centres
● Providing social work support and counselling and short periods of relief care
● Giving practical support in the home
● Giving advice on welfare rights

The SSD provides:

● Day care for children
● Day nurseries and family centres, including therapeutic work with children in need and their carers
● Accommodation for children who, with the agreement of their parents, need a period of care away from their family
● Care for children who are made the subject of a Care Order by the courts
● A range of services for children with disabilities, alongside the health and education services
● An adoption service

The SSD has a duty:

● To register and inspect childminders and all-day care facilities provided by voluntary and private organisations
● To investigate the circumstances of any child believed to be at risk of harm, and to take action on their behalf

Information about your local Social Services Department can be obtained from its offices (they are listed in the telephone directory or your local library). The SSD have leaflets to inform the public about their services.

NOW ANSWER THESE QUESTIONS

1 At what age must a child attend school in Britain?
2 What is the National Curriculum?
3 Which Act of Parliament gave local authorities a duty to provide services for children in need in their area?
4 What is meant by a 'child in need'?
5 Name one of the duties of the SSD.

45 Housing, Social Security and Health Services

Apart from education and social services, the main services provided by the state for children and their families are those involving the provision of housing, social security (money and benefits) and health. In each of these sectors there are a range of voluntary organisations that supplement the services provided by the state.

HOUSING

There are a range of financial benefits and allowances payable by the Department of Social Security through local Benefits Agency offices

Local authorities have a duty to provide housing for the people in their area and to ensure that families with dependent children are not homeless. Council housing has been provided since the beginning of the twentieth century, but since the early 1980s provision has decreased. People have been encouraged to buy their council houses, but councils are not allowed to build new houses with the money gained from sales. This has contributed to a rise in the number of homeless families.

Local authorities often place homeless families in hostels or in bed and breakfast accommodation. This is a very expensive and unsuitable form of provision.

Housing benefit is paid by local councils to people who need help to pay their rent. **Housing associations** provide an alternative to council housing. They are non-profit-making and exist to provide homes for people in need from different social and cultural backgrounds. They provide homes by building new units and improving or converting older properties. The government encourages the growth of housing associations and provides money for them through the **Housing Corporation**. You can find out about the housing associations in your area from your local **Community Volunteer Service**.

HEALTH

The **National Health Service (NHS)** was created in 1948 to give free health care to the entire population. The National Health Service and Community Care Act 1990 has led to the most recent series of reforms. This Act aimed to bring the 'marketplace' into the health service. This means that within the service there are some officers who are **purchasers** of services (e.g. GPs) and others who are **providers** of services (e.g. NHS Trusts). The main services provided for families are general practitioners, health visitors, midwives, child health clinics, district nurses, dentists and opticians and hospital services.

The **Department of Health** (central government) is in overall charge of planning the health service through **District Health Authorities**.

There are a wide range of voluntary organisations that help people with different medical conditions. Some are national, others are self-groups organised locally.

THE DEPARTMENT OF SOCIAL SECURITY

The aim of social security is to make sure that all adults have a basic income when they are unable to earn enough to keep themselves and their dependants. There are a range of financial benefits and allowances payable by the Department of **Social Security** through local **Benefits Agency** offices.

The Social Security Act 1986 set out the main recent changes that were introduced in April 1988:

BENEFIT TYPE	WHAT IT INCLUDES	WHO IS ELIGIBLE
Contributory benefits	Sickness, unemployment, disability, old age, maternity and widowhood benefits	Paid to people in particular categories providing they have previously made a contribution through National Insurance.
'Universal' non-contributory benefits	Child Benefit, payable to all mothers; One Parent Benefit, payable to all one-parent families, and Disability Living Allowance	A person has to be in a particular category, but does not have to have made a contribution previously. They can claim them, whatever their income.
'Means tested' non-contributory benefits	**Income Support:** Payable to people who are not in paid employment, or who are employed part-time, and on low incomes **Family Credit:** Paid to families when a parent works more than 16 hours a week but their income is below a certain level **The Social Fund:** Loans and payments are made from this to meet particular needs not covered by income support.	Only given to people in a certain category providing their income and savings are below a certain level. In order to claim, these people must fill in lengthy forms (tests) about their means (income), which can put them off.

CHARITIES

There are many charities that give financial assistance to people in need in different situations. People need first to be aware of these and then to put in an application stating their case (see *The Charities Digest*). The pressure on charities has increased recently and usually the demand exceeds the money available.

NOW ANSWER THESE QUESTIONS

1 Why has the number of council houses reduced in recent years?
2 What is a universal benefit?
3 What is a means test?
4 Who is eligible for income support?
5 Name three services provided for children by the NHS.

Voluntary and Private Services

There are a wide range of voluntary and private organisations that support families and children. These supplement the work of the statutory services. Addresses and further information can be obtained from *The Charities Digest* and under 'Voluntary Organisations' in the Yellow Pages directory.

NATIONAL VOLUNTARY ORGANISATIONS

- **Barnados** works with children and their families to help relieve the effects of disadvantage and disability. It runs community projects and day centres and provides residential accommodation for children with special needs.
- **ChildLine** provides a national telephone helpline for children in trouble or danger.
- **The Children's Society** offers child care services to children and families in need. It aims to help children to grow up in their own families and communities.
- **Citizens' Advice Bureaux** provide free, impartial advice and help to anyone. They have over a thousand local offices which provide information, advice and legal guidance on many subjects.
- **Contact a Family** promotes mutual support between families caring for disabled children. It organises community-based projects that assist parents' self-help groups, and runs a national helpline.
- **Family Service Units** provide a range of social and community work services and support to disadvantaged families and communities, with the aim of preventing family breakdown.
- **The Family Welfare Association** offers services for families, children and people with disabilities. It provides financial help for families in exceptional need, gives social work support and runs drop-in centres.
- **Gingerbread** provides emotional support, practical help and social activities for lone parents and their children.
- **Jewish Care** provides help and support for people of the Jewish faith and their families. Amongst other things, it runs day centres and provides social work teams and domiciliary (home) assistance.
- **Mencap** aims to increase public awareness

Contact a Family promotes mutual support between families caring for disabled children

of the problems faced by mentally handicapped people and their families. It supports day centres and other facilities.
- **MIND** is concerned with improving services for people with mental disorders and promoting mental health.
- **NCH** (National Children's Home) provides services for children who are disadvantaged. It runs many schemes including family centres, foster care and aid and support schemes for families.
- **The National Deaf Children's Society** is a national charity working specially for deaf children and their families. It gives information, advice and support directly to families with deaf children.
- **The National Society for the Prevention for Cruelty to Children** (NSPCC) has a network of child protection teams throughout Britain. The RSSPCC works similarly in Scotland. It runs a 24-hour referral and counselling telephone line, and offers support via family care centres.

- **Parentline** offers a telephone support helpline for parents who are having any kind of problem with their children.
- **Play Matters** (The National Toy Libraries Association) exists to promote awareness of the importance of play for the developing child. Libraries are organised locally, loaning toys to families with young children.
- **The Pre-School Learning Alliance** promotes the interests of playgroups at a local and national level.
- **RELATE** (The National Marriage Guidance Council) trains and provides counsellors to work with people who are experiencing difficulty in their relationships.
- **The Samaritans** offer a telephone befriending service to the despairing.
- **Women's Refuges** provide 'halfway houses' for women and children who are the victims of violent male partners until they can be re-accommodated.

LOCAL VOLUNTARY ORGANISATIONS AND PRIVATE SERVICES

In most areas there are a wide range of local voluntary organisations that have grown up to meet the needs of the local population. Some are self-help groups, others meet the needs of people from a variety of ethnic and national backgrounds. They may provide specific information services, advice and support. They are often listed and co-ordinated by a local Council for Voluntary Service and can be found under 'Voluntary Organisations' in Yellow Pages.

- **African-Caribbean.** Indian and Pakistani community centres exist in areas where there are significant numbers of people of Caribbean and Asian origin. They offer a range of advice and support services for local people. There are also a wide range of local organisations that aim to meet the needs of other minority communities.
- **Parent and toddler groups** sometimes use the same facilities. At these, carers can bring very young children, but are required to remain with them while they play.

Private provision

Some services are provided by private individuals and organisations to make a profit. They have identified a demand and people who are willing to pay for such services.

- **Personal services.** Some support services can be purchased privately – for example, personal and family therapy, different forms of counselling, domestic and care assistance. These services tend to be expensive and therefore beyond the means of many.
- **Childcare and education.** Nursery schools, day nurseries, crêches, nannies and child-minders all provide services that parents can purchase if they have the means to do so.
- **Housing.** There has been a steady rise in home ownership in recent years. However, only those with a steady income are able to raise and finance a mortgage.
- **Health services.** There has been a large growth in private sector provision since 1979, supported by the government. Increasingly, people who can afford to do so pay into private insurance schemes for private medical treatment. This usually means quicker treatment.
- **Finance/loans.** Those with steady jobs and capital assets are able to raise money through banks, building societies and reputable companies. However, families with few resources have to resort to expensive forms of borrowing, often through loan sharks who charge high rates of interest.

NOW ANSWER THESE QUESTIONS

1. Name three voluntary organisations that provide community services for children and their families.
2. What does the NSPCC do?
3. What is the role of Citizens' Advice Bureaux?
4. Where can you find out about voluntary organisations in an area?
5. Why do private services exist?

Review of Main Services

Private, state and voluntary organisations provide a range of child care and education services for young children. Their focus varies between education, substitute child care or a combination of both. They also differ in their hours of operation, cost, staffing and availability. Parents make their choices depending on how well the service meets their own and their children's needs, its cost and availability.

PRIVATE PROVISION				
PROVISION	**CLIENT GROUP**	**SERVICE**	**FUNDING**	**STAFFING**
Private preparatory schools	Education for children of school age whose parents choose to pay school fees	Education full-time in termtime	Parents' fees	Usually qualified teachers
Private nursery schools	Education for children whose parents choose to pay school fees	Educational experiences 5 x 6½ hours in termtime	Parents' fees	Many staff are teachers, but not all
Private day nurseries	Substitute childcare to free parental time for work etc.	Daytime care throughout the year for babies up to 5 years old, and some after-school clubs	Parents' fees (and possible government funding)	At least half staff should have a child care qualification
Workplace/ college crèches	Substitute childcare to free parental time for work or study	Care during the working day throughout the year or term for babies to five years and some after-school clubs	Often subsidised by employer or college plus parental fees.	Half of staff must be qualified
Childminders	Substitute childcare to free parental time for work etc.	Childcare in childminders' home; must be registered with Social Services; hours are negotiated	Parents' fees. Sometimes subsidised by a Social Services department	No qualifications required but must be 'fit persons'
Nannies	Substitute care or assisting parent at home	In child's own home (some families may share a nanny); daily or live-in	Wages paid by parents and may include board and lodging	No qualifications required

STATE PROVISION				
PROVISION	**CLIENT GROUP**	**SERVICE**	**FUNDING**	**STAFFING**
Infant or primary schools	Education of school-age children according to the National Curriculum	Full-time education 5 x 6½ hours in termtime	Public funds from taxes	Qualified teachers + class-room assts.
Reception classes	Education for 'rising fives'	Educational experiences 5 x 6½ hours in termtime	Public funds from taxes	As above
State-maintained nursery units	Education for 3–5-year-olds, usually in units attached to schools or in separate schools	Educational experiences 5 x 2½ hours in termtime	Public funds from taxes	Qualified teachers and child care workers
Local authority day nurseries and family centres	Care for children under five recognised as being 'in need' in that area, plus support for their families	Care during the working day throughout the year for babies up to five years (but sometimes only offered on a part-time sessional basis)	Public funding. There may be some payment of fees according to carer's ability to pay	Half **must** be qualified, but policy is often that **all** should be qualified.

VOLUNTARY PROVISION				
Family centres	Support for carers and care of their children	Care and stimulation of children and support for carers including help with parenting skills	Fundraising and government subsidy	Usually qualified staff
Play-groups	Learning through play for children from 2½ or 3, to 5 years	Varies according to area; usually 1 to 5 x 2½-hour sessions a week in termtime	Parents' fees, vouchers. Subsidised by low staff and rent costs	Local authority may require training for play leaders
Home visiting	Educational and social support for children in need and their carers	Visits at home for an hour every week or two to encourage play and care	Voluntary groups, or family centres supported by public funds	Volunteers must be shown to be 'fit persons'

NOW ANSWER THESE QUESTIONS

1. What are the three main sources of education and care provision for under-fives?
2. Name **two** types of childcare provision funded from parental fees.
3. Name **two** types of childcare provision funded from public funds.
4. During which hours would a child usually attend a state nursery school?
5. What services may be offered by a local authority day nursery?

A Positive Environment: Key Terms

You should now understand the following key terms. If you do not, go back through the previous chapter to find out.

Admission programme
Age-appropriate
  behaviour
Antecedent
Behaviour Modification
Children in need
Confidentiality
Department of Social
  Security
Discrimination
Discriminatory practices
Emotional maturity
Empowerment
Equality of opportunity
Ethnic group
Family diversity
Framework for
  children's behaviour

Goals and boundaries
Grief
Independence
Institutionalised
  discrimination
Legal and political
  framework
Local Authority
Multiple transitions
National Curriculum
National Health Service
Negative attitudes
Parental involvement
Partnership with
  parents
Prejudice
Private services
Racism

Role models
Self-esteem
Self-image
Self-identity
Social Services
  Department
Statutory services
Stereotypical
  assumptions
The Children Act 1989
Transitions
Values and norms
Voluntary organisations
Welfare State

PART 2

Course Assessment

4 PLANNING AND WRITING AN ASSIGNMENT

This chapter covers:
- Types of assignments
- Writing an introduction
- Presentation and effective documentation
- Research, making notes and references
- Equal Opportunities
- Conclusions
- Harvard system of referencing
- Bibliography
- Marking systems, using marking criteria and weighing marks

What is an assignment?

An assignment is any piece of written work which has been requested and involves planning and research. It could be evidence of under-pinning knowledge for NVQ assessment or a formal project for a CACHE course such as the Certificate in Child Care and Education.

Assignments may be subject-specific – i.e. linked to a particular subject area such as health or education – or they may integrate two or more areas. The CCE requires that all candidates produce one formal integrated assignment towards the end of the course which covers all areas of the syllabus studied during the one-year programme. This means that aspects of most or all of the 12 core modules will be tested. The purpose of this type of assignment is to allow candidates to demonstrate their knowledge and understanding of how they can competently care for children.

Remember that this is a national assignment: it is set by the Council for Awards in Children's Care and Education (CACHE), and all candidates throughout the country will be answering the same questions. There is a time-limit of six working weeks for completion set by each study centre. If you need an extension to the time-limit it must be negotiated individually, since granting an extension is at the discretion of each centre.

Most assignments will have more than one section. There may be many different sections, each with separate parts to be answered. These help candidates to answer effectively and structure their work. The separate questions may relate to particular areas of the syllabus.

Reading the question

Read the questions carefully and pick out key words.

Ask yourself: What is the question getting at? What does it really mean? What knowledge is this going to test? For example, look at this question:

'A six-year-old child with a chronic disability has recently been discharged from hospital. How can the nursery nurse support the child at home?'

This question is about care at home and not about how the nursery nurse at school may offer support to the child and family. A simple phrase like 'nursery nurse' may make you think the question relates to caring for children in a formal child care establishment. This type of question can seem to be misleading, but if you read the question carefully and underline the key words you will answer correctly. Do not assume things or jump to conclusions.

Planning your time

Below is a suggested plan for completing an assignment:

Week 1
- Read through the assignment carefully.
- Ask tutors for advice and suggestions, make notes.
- Plan timetable for completing assignment on time.
- Write to relevant organisations.

Week 2
- Research subject areas.
- Visit library and read books, magazines and journals related to assignment.

- Ask librarians for help, use microfiche, CD-ROM etc.
- Read newspapers and look for any topical coverage of subject area.
- Record details of all articles read during research and include in bibliography.
- Speak to placement supervisor about areas associated with placement.

Week 3
- As above, and continue reading and making notes.
- Record references and quotes.

Week 4
- Begin to answer questions in rough.
- Continue reading around subject areas.

Week 5
- Write up answers to questions.
- Compile list of references and bibliography.

Week 6
- Hand in completed assignment on or before due date. (Remember: work handed in late can only be awarded a pass mark, not a merit or distinction; nor can it be re-submitted if it is not up to standard.)

Presentation

Your aim should be to produce work that is neat, tidy, logically ordered and easy to read. Illegible work will be returned in order to give candidates the opportunity to improve the work.

- Assignments may be handwritten in ink (pencil is not acceptable), typed or word-processed. Use the spellcheck if word processing.
- Use A4 paper. However, if a booklet, pamphlet or other type of product is requested, any presentation which lends itself is acceptable.
- Include the completed and signed candidate work verification form. Write your comments relating to the assignment on this. For example, was it enjoyable? Has it helped you to assimilate your knowledge? Have you learned a lot from your research?
- Include the marking guidelines.
- Label each sheet with your name and PIN number.
- Include a contents list with page numbers for each section.
- Label each section and question clearly.
- Include a References and Bibliography section.

Writing an introduction

It is usually a good idea to write a brief introduction to your assignment if the word limit allows it. There may marks allocated for the introduction. It should set out the aim of the assignment and give a logical but concise outline of the way you intend to approach the assignment.

It may be easier to write the introduction *after* completing the bulk of the assignment. This sounds odd, but it is simpler to introduce what you have actually done than what you intend to do, because your ideas and plans may change as you proceed through the assignment.

Equal opportunities

The concept of equal opportunities must be 'embedded' into all pieces of work, including observations, plans and portfolio activities. Everyone who works with children should have a professional attitude based on accepting the differences between members of society, and on a refusal to tolerate discrimination of any kind, whether on grounds of gender, class, religion, race, culture, disability, age, etc. Despite the legislation against discrimination, some people still hold negative and prejudiced attitudes which should be challenged. Children find it difficult to confront prejudice and need an environment where they feel valued, so that they can develop high self-esteem and a feeling of self-worth.

Throughout any assignment, remember to include relevant information about equal opportunities. Try not to make 'token statements': read the Equal Opportunities Policy from your placement and try to incorporate it into your placement-related work by, for example:

- Meeting the individual needs of all children
- Checking books for race/gender bias
- Promoting positive images and role models of men and women, disability, cultural diversity, social class, age etc.
- Organising displays which reflect a multicultural society
- Allowing all the children to share their experiences and feel valued
- Encouraging boys and girls to sit together in mixed-gender groups

Marking criteria

When the assignments are distributed you should also receive a copy of the **marking criteria**. These tell you how many marks are allocated to each section/question and what you must do to achieve the marks. Keep the criteria in mind when writing the assignment (see page 108).

You may find that more marks are allocated to some sections than others, so you must decide how to achieve the best mark in each section.

If there is a word limit for the assignment, there may be a relationship between how many marks are available for each section and the number of words allowed. For example:

Overall word limit = 2,000 words

Section 1 = 10 marks = approx 200 words
Section 2 = 30 marks = approx 600 words
Section 3 = 40 marks = approx 800 words
Section 4 = 20 marks = approx 400 words

Total = 2,000 words

This is a very rough guide to allocating words for marks – but it does suggest that you should be writing more in a section worth 40 marks than in a section worth 20 marks.

Try to allocate words to marks as far as possible, bearing in mind that one handwritten side of A4 paper in average-sized writing equals roughly 250 words. Ten per cent above or below the word limit is generally acceptable, but study centres are entitled to refuse to mark work above this limit, so beware!

Remember that you must pass every section to achieve a pass mark overall.

Grading

Assignments are graded **Pass**, **Merit** or **Distinction**. Percentage marks for each grade are:

Pass = 50%
Merit = 65%
Distinction = 80%

Try to put an equal amount of effort into every section of the assignment. If you get distinction level in every question but one, and just fail that one, on re-submission you can only achieve an overall pass mark.

Harvard referencing

Writing an assignment will certainly involve reading books and articles to increase your knowledge and understanding of the subject. You will most probably find some ideas and/or opinions of others valuable and want to include them in your own assignment, either as a direct quote or in paraphrased form (i.e. repeating their ideas in your own words). This is quite acceptable and most people writing essays and assignments will refer to the work of others. However, it must be very clear to the reader which is your own work and which is the work of others and so you must acknowledge everything that is not your own original work.

This is done by **referencing**, i.e. giving details of the book or articles you have used in preparing your assignment. There are several acceptable ways of referencing but for CACHE assignments, the **Harvard** system of referencing is recommended. This involves listing the books, journals and articles referred to in the text alphabetically by the author's last name and initials, the date of publication, followed by the title of the work, the place of publication and the publisher. For example:

> Beaver, M. *et al.* (1995): *Babies and Young Children*, Book 2: Work and Care. Cheltenham: Stanley Thornes

If you are referencing a magazine or journal article you must include the author of the article, the title of the article, the name of the journal or magazine, the issue number or date of publication and the page(s) referred to. For example:

> Brewster, J (1997): 'Care of the Sick Child', *Nursery World* March 1997, pp13–17

> Brewster, J (1997) 'Care of the Sick Child' *Nursery World* 121, 53, p16

When referring to ideas in the text you can use the following format:

> '...Beaver *et al.* (1995, pp50–1) suggest that adults have a valuable role in planning play activities for children, and that they should prepare, interact and observe the children to ensure that they gain the maximum benefit from the activity...'

– or you can quote directly, in which case the passage should be indented from the main text of the assignment by increasing the margin:

> 'Adults have an important role in children's play to ensure that the maximum benefit is gained... from it. The adult needs to plan and prepare the activities carefully. They also need to interact... with the children during the activity and monitor what is happening through observation.'

> (Beaver *et al.*, 1995, p50)

There may be books and articles which you have read which you do not refer to directly in your work. However it is still important to make clear that you have read around the subject. These should be listed alphabetically by the author's last name in the bibliography.

There are easy marks to be gained from producing a good and sound list of references and a bibliography, so it is certainly worth compiling it alphabetically. Make sure that all the material referred to is relevant and reflects a wide range of reading and research.

Plagiarism

Plagiarism means taking and using another person's thoughts and writing as your own. It is very important to include a reference for every idea or quote you use in your assignment. If you quote directly, you must use quotation marks and give a precise reference to the source.

Use your own words to set out the argument for an assignment. If you try to pass off other people's work as your own – and this includes the work of other candidates on the course – it will be treated as an attempt to cheat, and the work will become null and void:

> Cheating in assignments is defined as 'representing as one's own work the work of others'. This includes submitting an assignment or part of an assignment which has been written jointly with other persons or has been copied in its entirety or in part, without acknowledgement from the work of other persons, including that appearing as published material.

The Open University

Writing a conclusion

To pull all your ideas and arguments together, it is a good idea to provide a short paragraph concluding the sections and/or assignment (whichever is appropriate). This should not contain any new information but should aim to present a short summary of the main points. A conclusion should:

- Be presented logically – i.e. summarise points in the order in which they appear in the assignment or section
- Relate directly to the content of the section/assignment
- State whether the aims of the section have been achieved
- Evaluate what you have researched
- Outline how the assignment has extended your learning

Shown on pages 109–10 are some guidelines for the 1996 integrated assignment for candidates completing the CACHE Certificate in Child Care and Education. Reading these and relating them to the sample assignment on page 108 may help you to prepare to write an assignment. Good luck!

1996 Integrated Assignment
'Play is central to the young child's development'

Section 1

Describe a play setting which includes both indoor and outdoor areas for children aged between 1–3 years OR 4–7 years 11 months (*15 marks*)

Section 2

a) What provision should be made in the play setting to encourage equality of opportunity? (*10 marks*)

b) What health and safety factors should be taken into account when planning a play setting? (*10 marks*)

Section 3

Select one play/learning area and explain how it can promote the all-round development of the child. (*10 marks*)

Section 4

a) When and how should adults intervene in children's play? (*10 marks*)

b) How can the child care and education worker work with parents/carers to enhance the children's play experience? (*10 marks*)

c) Suggest three organisations which would be of value to the child and parent and briefly describe their role. (*10 marks*)

Section 5

EITHER Design a leaflet/information sheet which explains to a parent/carer the importance of play to the young child's development.

OR Give a 5–10-minute oral presentation which explains the importance of play to the young child's development. (*10 marks*)

Marking allocation

Presentation	*10 marks*
Section 1	*15 marks*
Section 2	*20 marks*
Section 3	*10 marks*
Section 4	*30 marks*
Section 5	*10 marks*
References and bibliography	*5 marks*
TOTAL	*100 marks*

Pass	50%
Merit	65%
Distinction	80%

Sample assignment and marking scheme

CACHE CERTIFICATE IN CHILDCARE AND EDUCATION
1996 ASSIGNMENT GUIDELINES

Presentation

Refer to the assignment guidelines.
1   Put name, group number and PIN on the front cover.
2   Use a small plastic folder. Do not use plastic wallets/envelopes or ring-binders.
3   Number pages in the top right-hand corner.
4   Use dividers to separate sections. You will need six.

Section 1
● Select an age-group, e.g. 1–2, 3–5, 1–4, 4–7, 5–7 etc.
● Your entire assignment will relate to this age-group of children.
● Write a description of an indoor and an outdoor play setting for your chosen age-group.
● You should use a minimum of 500 words for each.

You may produce a plan/diagram to illustrate your description. A description to include detail of activities/equipment provided, e.g. more detail than 'painting area' – to include types of brushes, types of paper, opportunities for children to mix paint, use sponges, cotton buds etc. Outdoor area should include: equipment for climbing, wheeled toys, toys to encourage co-operative play (especially for under-5s), grassed area, plants, trees, bushes, area for gardening, seating.

Section 2
The play setting should be the same as Section 1.

A   Under the Children Act 1989 there is a requirement to recognise children's individuality with reference to reflecting the multicultural community. Children's special and individual needs should also be catered for. Play should be non-gender-specific.

● Responding to individuality: range of difficulty of books, jigsaws, games, etc. Choices of activities
● Disability: not just ramps. Equipment to help children with poor hand control, Velcro on dressing-up clothes etc.
● Gender: books/jigsaws with girls as main character, range of dressing-up clothes, opportunities for all children to have access to equipment
● Ethnicity: reflected in display, notices, home corner equipment, books, stories, songs and music, jigsaws etc.
● Social background: range of equipment/resources reflecting different family situations

B   Link to play setting in Section 1.

● Cover indoor and outdoor areas.
● You may produce a plan to show where safety factors need to be considered, or use the plan from the previous section if you have made one.
● Write a commentary on A4 paper to justify these factors.

Alongside health and safety factors – awareness of accountability to parents and criteria laid down by guiding standards, issued by social services, should be evident.
May include: ventilation, floor space and floor coverings, adult/child ratios, doors with high handles and controlled closure, windows, access to other areas of setting, toilets, kitchen area, safety marks on equipment, safety glass, protected radiators, access to water in relevant areas etc.
Outdoor areas with safe surfaces under climbing equipment, secure fencing and gates etc.

Section 3
● Age-group the same.
● Choose any area, indoors or outdoors.
● Refer to each area of development, use PILES or SPLICES.*
● Refer to theory – use references.

Continued on page 110

Continued from page 109

Section 3

A and B: Answer in essay form using at least 500 words for each.
Refer to theory.
Link to chosen age-group.

A Intervention

How

- Provide an extension to the play or change where the play is taking place.
- Re-organise nursery/classroom – management
- Ensure children understand organisation and routine of the establishment.
- Establish necessary rules for use of equipment and materials.
- Remind children of these rules periodically.
- Be an arbitrator in quarrels.
- Participate in play.
- Initiate play.

When

- When children appeal for help – orally and with gestures (non-verbal communication)
- Problems which cannot be resolved by children themselves
- Disruption of play
- Equipment being misused
- Children in danger
- Interference by children with other activities, e.g. rushing around, noise, using too much space in the establishment
- As infrequently as possible – only when children cannot cope alone with resolution of an issue around the play
- When play becomes purposeless and children need ideas to re-invigorate it

B

Good communication systems between home and child care environment
Clear statement of school/nursery purpose, e.g. learning through play
Willingness to explain and demonstrate
Publicise availability of resources e.g. toy library, playbus etc.

C

Some ideas to choose from but you may think of others:

- Toy library
- Library services
- Social services
- Health centres
- Leisure centres
- Playgroups
- Parent and toddler groups
- Voluntary organisations

Write a short paragraph explaining the value of a particular organisation to a child and their parent/carer. Evidence of research will be required, e.g. a leaflet or letter from the organisation.

Sections 5 and 6

Refer to the assessment guidelines.
References must include the author's last name and the year of publication in the text.
Produce an alphabetical list by author, book, date, publisher, place of publication.

*   PILES = **P**hysical, **I**ntellectual, **L**inguistic, **E**motional, **S**ocial
    SPLICES = **S**ocial, **P**hysical, **L**inguistic, **I**ntellectual, **C**ultural, **E**motional, **S**piritual

5 PORTFOLIO BUILDING

> **This chapter covers:**
> - Principles of portfolio building
> - Portfolios for National Vocational Qualifications (NVQ)
> - Portfolios for Certificate in Child Care and Education (CCE)

To achieve an NVQ or the CCE and other qualifications, you need to compile a **portfolio of evidence**.

A portfolio is a file where you will keep the evidence of your ability to work competently with children. The evidence in a portfolio can be in different forms, e.g. child observations, logs, accounts of activities, assessor observations, audio- and videotapes and other authenticated evidence of competent practice.

It is important to arrange your portfolio in a logical way so that the assessor and verifier are able to confirm that the evidence in the portfolio supports your claim that you are a competent candidate.

NVQs in Child Care and Education

NVQs in Child Care and Education are offered at Level 2 and Level 3. These qualifications are validated by different awarding bodies but every awarding body will expect a candidate's portfolio to contain:

- Name and address
- Candidate registration number
- Name of approved assessment centre
- A statement about you. This could include a curriculum vitae.
- A brief description of your place of work/training
- Observation/log sheets completed by your assessor
- Element Assessment Record sheets (EARs)
- Unit summary sheets
- Qualification summary sheet
- Evidence to support competent practice

Every candidate undertaking an NVQ will have an **assessor** who will guide and support them in building a portfolio. Your assessor will also complete log sheets, Element Assessment Record sheets, Unit Summary sheets and Qualification Summary sheets and give you copies of these to store in your portfolio.

UNIT SUMMARY SHEET
Unit E2: Maintain the safety of children

Elements:
E.2.1 Maintain a safe environment for children ☐
E.2.2 Maintain supervision of children ☐
E.2.3 Carry out emergency procedures ☐
E.2.4 Cope with accidents and injuries to children ☐
E.2.5 Help keep children safe from abuse ☐
E.2.6 Ensure children's safety on outings ☐

Competence has been demonstrated in all of the elements in this Unit through the agreed assessment procedures

	Name (block capitals)	Signature	Date
Assessor			
	Name (block capitals)	Signature	Date
Internal verifier			

I am satisfied with the way the assessment(s) was conducted and with its outcome

	Name (block capitals)	Signature	Date
Candidate			
Candidate registration No.			

Name of approved assessment centre

Element Assessment Record Sheet.

Unit Nº & Title:
C.2 CARE FOR CHILDREN'S PHYSICAL NEEDS
Element Nº & Title:
C.2.3 Respond to illness in a child

	Performance Criteria Nº	Log Entry Nº		Evidence Gathering Methods
		Page Nº	Nº	
1				
2				
3				
4				
5				
6				
7				
8				
9				

Key: A = Direct Observation B = Questioning
C = Interrogation/ rationale D = Work Plans
E = Inspection of setting F = Reflective accounts
G = Log books/ diaries H = Plans
I = Case studies/ assignments J = Child Observations
K = Sim/ role play sit. rehearsal L = Analogue evidence
M = Prior achievement

Methods used for this element were ? (tick methods used)
Overall A B C D E F G H I J K L M
Knowledge A B C D E F G H I J K L M

Range

	Log Entry Nº	Evidence Gathering Methods
Types of illness:		
minor ailments and discomfort		
sudden acute illness		
unconsciousness		
Age band:		
1 to 4 years		
4 to 7 years		
Characteristics of children:		
children with communication difficulties		
children without communication difficulties		

Special Notes
Direct observation of performance in the workplace especially with regard to C.2.3.2.
C.2.3.4, C.2.3.7.

Candidate's Name :
Signature :
Assessor's Name :
(Please Print)
Signature :

EVIDENCE LOG SHEET

Page No.

Entry Number & Date	Evidence Gathering Method	Entry (Note: Please sign and date all entries)	Unit and Element Reference

Candidate's Name: Candidate Registration Number:

Sample Unit Summary sheet, Element Assessment Record (EAR) sheet and Evidence Log sheet

Each NVQ award in Child Care and Education is divided into:

- Core units
- Endorsement units

At Level 2 there are 8 core units to be completed by all candidates:

- Unit C2: Care for children's physical needs
- Unit C4: Support for children's social and emotional development
- Unit C6: Contribute to the management of children's behaviour
- Unit C8: Set out and clear away children's play activities
- Unit C9: Work with young children
- Unit E1: Maintain a child-oriented environment
- Unit E2: Maintain the safety of children
- Unit P2: Establish and maintain relationships with parents of young children

To complete their awards at Level 2, candidates must complete one endorsement (each endorsement consists of two units). These can be chosen from a range, and candidates will normally select the endorsement which relates to their area of work.

Endorsements at Level 2 are:

- Endorsement A: Work with babies
  Unit C12: Feed babies
  Unit C13: Care for babies
- Endorsement B: Work in support of others
  Unit M1: Give administrative and technical support on request
  Unit M3: Work under the direction of others
- Endorsement C: Work in a pre-school group
  Unit P9: Work with parents in a group for young children
  Unit M2: Carry out the administration for the provision of a child care and education setting
- Endorsement D: Work in a community-run pre-school group
  Unit P9: Work with parents in a group for young children
  Unit M20: Work with/to a management committee

The letter of the unit title (e.g. 'E1') relates to the area of practical competence being assessed:

- **C** units relate to children.
- **E** units relate to the environment.
- **P** units relate to parents.
- **M** units relate to management.

How to arrange your portfolio

There is no right or wrong way to arrange a portfolio. Each candidate will develop their own ideas about the best way to present their evidence. The important thing to remember is that other people, especially your assessor and internal verifier, will need to be able to use your portfolio. They must satisfy themselves that your evidence proves that you are a competent candidate, so whatever system you use, you must make it easy for them to do this. A good contents page is vital to identify the evidence in your portfolio by page number or by section and page number.

Here are some suggestions that you might develop.

Basic information
Begin your portfolio with this basic information:

- A contents page to show what your portfolio contains
- Your name and address
- Your registration number/PIN (personal identification number) from the awarding body
- The name and number of your assessment centre
- Your personal statement and CV
- Information about your workplace
- Records of any skill checks, self-assessments, interviews or planning which was done to help you get started on your award
- A specimen signature of any person who signs evidence in your portfolio
- Records of self-assessments, skill checks, planning

At this point you will need to decide if you are going to divide your portfolio into sections. The easiest way to do this is to have a section for each unit. So for Level 2 your portfolio will have 10 sections.

Arranging a portfolio section
In each section include:

- A contents page for the unit
- The unit summary sheet for the unit
- The EAR sheet for each element of the unit
- Assessor log sheets and feedback sheets relating to the unit
- Your evidence relating to the unit

Evidence
Evidence of your ability to practise competently needs to be included in your portfolio. Much of this evidence will be gathered when your

assessor observes you in the normal working situation. This is called 'A evidence' and will be recorded by the assessor on the assessor log sheet. Your assessor may also ask you questions. This is called 'B evidence' and will be recorded in a similar way.

You may collect other evidence which the assessor can use to judge that you are competent. This evidence comes in different forms, e.g. activity plans, observations and extracts from your log or diary. Your assessor will guide you when you are planning assessments so that you will know what evidence you can present in this way to supplement their observations.

When you put your evidence into a section in your portfolio you need to label it with:

● The page number in the portfolio
● The unit and element number to which it relates

This will enable the assessor to cross-reference your evidence to the assessor log sheets. This is very important as it will enable anyone examining your portfolio to find evidence quickly and easily. You can also cross-reference evidence to other units in your portfolio.

You may decide not to divide your portfolio into unit sections but to have larger, more general sections. One way to do this would be to have sections for:

● Assessment records (e.g. unit summary sheets, EAR sheets, etc.)
● Your evidence

It is very important to number each page in the portfolio and to have a comprehensive contents section. Your evidence should also be clearly labelled with the number of the unit and element it relates to.

Before you decide how to present your portfolio, discuss it with your assessor and let them advise you on the best method. The way your assessor and verifier work may also influence your choice of method.

Bibliography
You could include a bibliography and reference section at the end of your portfolio. A bibliography is a way of listing books, articles, leaflets or any other materials that you have used while working for your award. The simplest way to do this is to make an alphabetical list with the author's name and initials first, the date of publication, followed by the title of the book and the publisher. For example:

Brown, B (1993): *All Our Children*, BBC Publications

The Certificate in Child Care and Education (CCE)

The Certificate in Child Care and Education is validated by the Council for Awards in Children's Care and Education (CACHE). The qualification is divided into 12 core modules and 4 option modules which are closely linked with the units in NVQ Child Care and Education Level 2.

Core modules in the Certificate in Child Care and Education are:

Module 1: Equality of Opportunity
Module 2: The Care and Education Environment
Module 3: Child Safety
Module 4: The Physical Care of the Developing Child
Module 5: Provision of Food and Drinks
Module 6: Childhood Illness
Module 7: Working with Young Children
Module 8: Play and the Young Child
Module 9: Emotional and Social Development
Module 10: Parents and Carers
Module 11: Managing Children's Behaviour
Module 12: Early Years' Services

To complete the award, candidates must complete one option. Each option consists of two modules:

Option 1: Work with Babies
Module 1a: Caring for Babies
Module 1b: Feeding Babies

Option 2: Skills for Employment
Module 2a: Working for Others
Module 2b: Administrative and Technical Support

The regulations linked to the CCE produced by CACHE will be used by your tutor to guide you.

The portfolio file required for the CCE is a record of work completed in practical placements. The portfolio is closely linked to the Practice Evidence Record sheets (PERs). These provide a record of:

- Placements attended
- Activities and observations completed
- Competencies achieved

The portfolio is a record of your work in practical placement. You will need a large file and some dividers to separate the sections of your portfolio. It is very important to organise your portfolio in a logical way. You should include:

- A contents page to show what your portfolio contains
- A signature sheet with the name, position and a specimen signature of anyone who signs your PER. For example:

SIGNATURE SHEET FOR PLACEMENT TRAINERS AND SUPERVISORS		
Name and type of placement (e.g. day nursery, nursery school etc.)	Supervisor's name	Supervisor's signature

You should also number all the pages in your portfolio and label each section.

The sections in your portfolio

You will need the following sections:

- Contents page or section
- **Personal details:** This should include your name, personal identification number (PIN), and the name and number of your study centre.
- Placements attended
- Type of placement, age-range of the children, staff, number of days attended
- **Portfolio activities:** These are the observations and activities listed in the PER. You may find it useful to separate observations from activities, especially if you intend to take the Diploma in Nursery Nursing at a later date.
- **Evidence of practical work:** This is a written record of events, tasks and activities that you have participated in. For example, you might include an account of an outing which you helped to plan.
- **Other evidence:** This consists of other relevant material collected during your practice. It could include leaflets, examples of records, examples of letters to parents and placement booklets.

- **Diary/log:** Although this is not compulsory, your tutor may advise you to keep a log or diary. This is simply a record of significant activities, events, situations in which you have been involved during your practical placement. Make your record brief but accurate. Remember to date your account and ask a responsible person to sign it. This will authenticate your evidence, so that you can use it for your PER.
- **References and bibliography:** Include a list of books and references used during your training (see pages 107 and 115).

Cross-referencing work to the PER

It is very important to use page numbers in your portfolio so that you can cross-reference your work to the PER. For example, if you have written an account of an outing on pages 10, 11, 12 of your portfolio, you can cross-reference to your PER by writing the page numbers in the space provided (see page 119 opposite)

Page numbering

You may want to number all the pages from the beginning to the end of your portfolio. An alternative is give each section a letter, e.g. A, B, C, etc. and start each section at page 1. This is useful because it allows you to number your portfolio as you go along, but it does mean that each section needs to have its own contents page.

For example, section B may have pages 1–20. To cross-reference a piece of work on page 4 in this section to your PER, you would write 'B4' in the space provided.

Whichever method you choose, you need to make certain that anyone examining your portfolio can find individual pieces of work quickly and easily.

Bibliography and references

At the end of your portfolio you should include a record of the books and references that you have used while working for your award. You will find details of how to organise this on page 115. You will also find examples of books that you could use listed in the Further Reading section on page 207.

The portfolio that you build for an NVQ or CCE award is a lasting record of your practice which you may be able to use when you progress to other qualifications such as The Diploma in Nursery Nursing, NVQ Child Care and Education Level 3. It is also useful to refer to when preparing for job interviews and will allow prospective employers to see evidence of your practical competence.

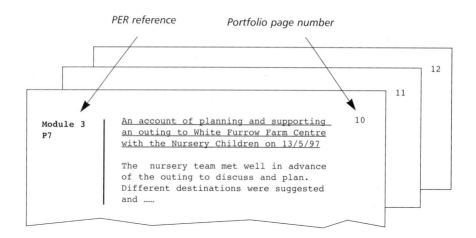

PER reference   Portfolio page number

Module 3
P7

An account of planning and supporting
an outing to White Furrow Farm Centre
with the Nursery Children on 13/5/97

The nursery team met well in advance
of the outing to discuss and plan.
Different destinations were suggested
and ......

10

11

12

Practice Evidence Record Sheet
Module 3 – Child Safety – Certificate
Range: 1–7 years 11 months

Candidate's Name   A. Brown   Candidate's PIN no.   35

Nos.	The candidate is able to:	Portfolio page	Signature of Tutor/Supervisor	Date
E2.6.1	1. Select or participate in the selection and planning of an outing that is appropriate to the age and stage of development of the child/children.	10	J. Smith	4/4/97
E2.6	2. Support an outing with other adults with either an individual child OR a small group of children OR a large group of children	11		
E2.6	3. Use the outing as a learning experience for the child/children	12		
E2.6	4. Assist in maintaining the supervision of the child/children on outings to ensure their safety			

Additional Evidence

Portfolio pages (top) cross-referenced to a Practice Evidence Record (PER) sheet (below)

6 UNDERSTANDING MULTIPLE CHOICE QUESTIONS

> **This chapter covers:**
> - Preparation hints
> - Planning your time
> - The structure of an MCQ question
> - Exam advice

Passing an MCQ exam

As a method of assessment, multiple choice questions, or 'MCQs', have both advantages and disadvantages for the student. An MCQ examination is used as part of the final assessment of the CACHE Certificate in Child Care and Education. If you are a student facing this or any other MCQ examination, be positive, concentrate on the advantages and read this chapter.

Remember that according to statistical probability, a monkey filling in the answers randomly would only get a quarter of the answers right – definitely not good enough for you!

Good preparation is the key to passing the exam. Effective preparation for an MCQ examination is the only way to guarantee success. You will be successful if you prepare.

Preparation hints

1 **Know your subject.** Preparation starts from the day you begin your course. There is no substitute for solid, consistent work throughout a course. This includes listening and participating in classes and lectures, thinking about what you are learning, asking questions when you do not understand, making clear notes and keeping them in good order in a file, together with any other written information you are given. Some MCQs are factual. If you concentrate throughout the course, you will have no problem in answering them correctly.

2 **Apply your knowledge to practice.** Some MCQs concern what should be done in a particular situation. This means you must have

both knowledge and understanding, and be able to apply it in practice. By working hard in your practical placements you will build up your professional skills and this will help you in the exam.

A word of warning. You need to be aware of *good* practice and use this as the basis of your answer. Sometimes you may observe practice that is less than ideal. If an answer to an MCQ is based on this observation, the answer will not be correct.

3   **Familiarise yourself with the different styles of question.** MCQs are written in different styles. The more familiar you are with these different styles, the more likely you are to be successful. Different styles are discussed later in this chapter. Familiarity helps to prevent the panic that many students feel when they are in a formal examination situation.

4   **Practise answering questions.** The saying 'practice makes perfect' certainly applies to MCQs. This book will help you to practise. Your lecturers will also help you. CACHE may supply a practice paper to your college. Good MCQs take a long time to write, so new questions can be in short supply. One solution is to try to write questions yourself in a class group, pool them and test each other on them. This can be fun. It makes you look at the syllabus and also makes you realize just how difficult question-writing really is!

5   **Revise thoroughly.** Start your revision early. Write a timetable for yourself so that you know when you will revise each subject. Do a little at a time and you are more likely to remember it. If you have listened and understood during the course, made good notes and filed them systematically, revision should be no problem for you. However, none of us is perfect, and this book is designed to help you to revise. It covers the syllabus, and can be used to guide your revision. Use it together with your own notes and any other books it refers to, or that you have used yourself during the course. If you combine this information with what you have learned in practice, you will pass.

The pros and cons of MCQs

Earlier we advised you to concentrate on the advantages of MCQs. What are they?

Well, there is certainly less risk of writer's cramp! You also know that the correct answer is in front of you – you just have to decide which one it is. But there are some disadvantages. You may feel apprehensive about having to remember a year's work for a final exam. Many students experience anxiety and most of them pass their exams without any trouble. You may have experienced modular assessment that did not involve MCQs. But you can succeed if you follow the hints in this chapter.

To pass an MCQ exam you need to know your facts and how to apply them to good practice. This is as it should be: after all, you are gaining a professional qualification to work with children, and this knowledge and understanding are the tools of your trade.

Many people find it a little nerve-racking to sit a formal examination. It is natural to be nervous. If your college can organize a mock exam in the same setting and under exam conditions this will help you to overcome some of your nerves. It also helps to have a good night's sleep beforehand and to be calm and collected on the day.

Planning your time

You have 60 minutes to complete the MCQ examination for CACHE and the paper has 40 questions. Most candidates find they have plenty of time, but students whose home language is not English sometimes need more time than others. This is because some questions are written with a structure that can present more difficulty to bilingual students, despite every effort on the part of the examiners to avoid it.

How long should you spend on each question?
The duration of 60 minutes for the paper means that you have 1 minute and 30 seconds to answer each question. Most candidates find that they can answer a proportion of questions correctly in less time than this. They may answer some in a very short time – perhaps as little as 30 seconds. Every time this happens to you, you have a full extra minute to answer another question that you may find more difficult. This means that, without running out of time, you could take as long as three minutes answering some questions. So never rush.

But do keep a regular eye on the time. You can use your own watch as long as you note your starting time and check that it is the same as the clock in the room or hall. Your invigilator should make sure that everyone can see a clock. They should also make a record of the start time and give occasional reminders of the time during the exam.

What if you do not know the answer?
If you have spent all your available time thinking about a question and still cannot decide on the answer, make an informed guess. Never leave an answer blank. At the very worst, you have a one in four chance of getting the answer right. If you use your knowledge, you should be able to reduce these odds. Go for the best option rather than nothing at all.

Ambiguous questions

An ambiguous question is one whose meaning is not clear and is open to more than one interpretation. Questions like this should not be on the paper. The awarding body, CACHE, makes every attempt to write good, clear questions that can only be interpreted in one way. It has an extended system of writing, checking, editing, pre-testing, re-editing and re-writing questions. Despite this, you may think a question is ambiguous. If so, do your best to work out what the question is trying to test and answer accordingly. Occasionally a question may be removed from the final exam score.

Understanding question structure

The question (stem)

The **stem** is the technical name for the part of the multiple choice that sets the question. Stems are written at different levels of difficulty and test different levels of knowledge and understanding.

The easiest level of stem tests knowledge of facts. For example:

a) What is normal body temperature?
b) Which foods are rich in vitamin A?
c) Which department must a childminder register with?

Some stems are slightly more difficult as they test knowledge and also require candidates to show understanding. For example:

a) Infant children will be most interested in a display table that includes...
b) The main difference between a statutory and a voluntary organisation is...
c) What are the MAIN reasons that children are more at risk as pedestrians than adults?

The most difficult stems require candidates to apply both knowledge and understanding to practice.
For example:

a) What are the MOST significant ways that a child care and education worker can support a child who has recently lost a parent?
b) How can a child care and education worker BEST ensure the safety of children in an outdoor play area?
c) A child of two years has tried to do a puzzle but suddenly throws it on the floor. The BEST action a child care and education worker can take is to...

Each exam paper will have a mixture and balance of these types of questions. Occasionally even the more able students make mistakes on some of the more difficult questions. They seem to see that many answers could be right if the question is approached in a certain way. These students should try to think about the question in a simple and straightforward way. Remember that the questions are never *deliberately* written to trick or mislead.

Capital letters

You will notice that in some of the stems a word is written in CAPITAL LETTERS. When you see this you need to pay close attention to the word. Read the stem again to yourself, putting emphasis on THAT word before you attempt to answer the question.

The answer (key and distractors)

The questions you answer will only have one correct answer. The technical name for the correct answer is the **key**. The key is always one of four possible options offered to you. The technical name for the three other possible, but incorrect, options is the **distractors**. (You do not need to remember these technical names, but it may help you to refer to them, especially if you try to write and share your own questions.)

Your task when answering a question is to find the key and discard the distractors. There are different ways you can do this, some of which depend on how the question is written. But however the question is presented, you must read the stem thoroughly first.

Techniques for finding the key

There is a choice of techniques for finding the key:

1 **Read the stem but do not look at the answers.** Try to think of the correct answer from your own knowledge. Then look at the options provided. See if one of them is the answer that you thought of. If it is, there is a good possibility that this is the key and you are correct. This is not a foolproof method, but if you use it for a few factual questions it will boost your confidence to tackle the more difficult ones. This method is more difficult to use for complex questions where you cannot predict the answers provided. But you can always start by trying this method.

2 Another way is to **read the stem, then read all the options carefully**. Think carefully, try to recall what you have learned and revised during the course, decide which one is correct. Check, then mark your answer sheet.

3   Finally, you can read the stem, read all the options carefully but **avoid making a quick decision.** If you are uncertain, read the options again, this time putting a cross on the question paper next to any answer that you know is a distractor. Do this again until you have eliminated three options. Check that you agree with the answer you have not crossed.

Following good practice

Use good practice as a guide. Remember that questions about what you should do in a specific situation are asking you about what is accepted as good practice *now*. Do not be distracted by answers based on what happened to you as a child. Remember that the accepted approach to children now is that they are developing individuals who need to be nurtured, stimulated, praised and valued. This has not always been so. You may have had personal experience of poor practice. You may find that some of the distractors are examples of what were once considered acceptable ways to treat children, but are no longer. Or you may have personally observed poor practice during your placement. Do not use this as a basis for answering your questions. For example:

> **Q.** A child of two has tried to do a puzzle but suddenly throws it on the floor. The BEST action you can take is to:
>
> a)   Tell the child he is naughty, must pick the puzzle up, and cannot play any more
> b)   Insist the child picks up every piece before he can play again
> c)   Encourage the child to help you to pick up the pieces and quietly lead him to another less demanding activity
> d)   Make an example of the child in front of the other children and ask them what he has done wrong

Hopefully you can see that (c) is the key. Unfortunately you may have experienced or witnessed some of the other alternatives being used.

To answer this question correctly, you need to understand the developmental stage of a two-year-old, normal behaviour at that age and the causes of it, and how to respond to a child's behaviour at that stage of development. This question is testing your knowledge of all these things and your ability to apply it. MCQs are not superficial!

Different question formats

In some questions there may be more than four options to choose from. There may be six to eight possible answers grouped together in four different combinations. For example:

Q: A typical child of one year will be MOST likely to display the following social behaviour:

1. Be generally sociable with any adult who is friendly
2. When requested, will wait for their needs to be met
3. Will probably have a particular friend
4. Will show a preference to be with a known adult
5. May be shy with strangers
6. May show rage if thwarted

a) 1, 2, 3
b) 2, 3, 5
c) 3, 4, 6
d) 4, 5, 6

In order to find the key, you have to select three correct answers and leave three distractors. What is the best way to arrive at the correct answer? There are a number of possible methods. You can:

1. Read the stem, then read all the answers carefully before making your choice
2. Initially ignore (a)–(d) above.
   - Read through 1–6 and put a cross beside any answer that you know to be false.
   - See if you have three answers uncrossed.
   - Check whether these three match any combination of numbers in (a)–(d).
   - Re-check the answers that are included in this combination and be sure that you agree with them.
   - Mark this answer on your answer sheet. Did you arrive at (d)?

You could do it the other way around – i.e. look at the combinations offered and decide which one you most agree with. But this can be confusing. You may become muddled and find it more difficult to decide which is the correct key. Only use this method as a last resort.

A good check is to decide if there is any answer that you know is definitely wrong. You will then know that any combination in which this is included cannot be the key. This will eliminate one or two distractors and/or confirm the decision you arrived at by Method 1 above.

There are other forms of questions where there are more than four answers to select from, perhaps in the form of a table or grid. These are similar to the questions above, but in this case the combinations of keys and distractors are grouped together visually in order to help you. You should not be put off by grids. Remember that they are designed to make things clearer for you, not more confusing. For example:

Q. Which of the following natural and manufactured materials would be good to use for creative play in a nursery?

a)	A selection of berries	A selection of seeds	Some unusual leaves	Bits of material
b)	Empty cereal boxes	Coloured paper	A selection of berries	Some unusual leaves
c)	Clean food containers	Bits of material	A selection of seeds	Some unusual leaves
d)	Empty cereal boxes	Coloured paper	Clean food containers	Bits of material

When you answer this question you could go through each row and cross out anything that would *not* be suitable for creative play with young children. The question leaves you to decide how to define 'good'. To define this you need to know that consideration must be given to size, practicality and attractiveness to the child, together with health and safety issues.

This should enable you to give (d) as the correct answer.

In the exam

Recording your answers

You will be given an answer sheet to record your answers. You must use an HB pencil and make your mark clearly in the space indicated. A sample answer sheet is shown on page 129 opposite.

The current practice is for candidates to make a small clear mark beside the letter that they think is the correct answer. It is important to mark it clearly – some students make such a faint mark it is almost impossible to see. The answer sheets are optically scanned and marked by computer. If the computer cannot see your mark it will record a void, which is the same as a wrong answer. Make sure that your mark is beside the correct question number. If you get this wrong, the result could be disastrous!

A word of warning. Never be tempted to change your answer because you have marked three or more of the same letter in a row (e.g. three 'a's or three 'b's etc.) The sequence of letters is random, and there could be as many as six answers in a row with the same letter.

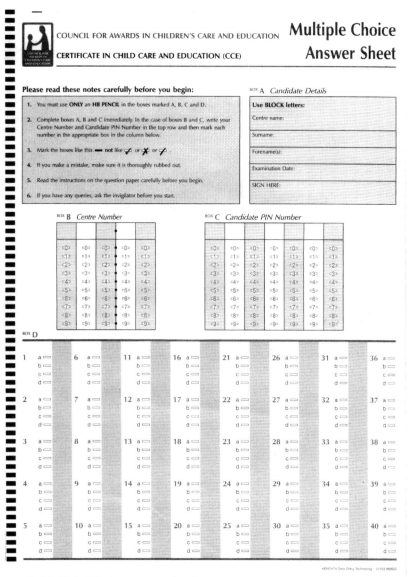

A sample Multiple Choice answer sheet

Things to take with you into the exam

You will be asked to take your PIN number (or other registration number if you are not taking a CACHE exam) to put on the front of your answer sheet. Do not forget this. You may be able to find your number out from the invigilator, but doing this will call attention to you, and will probably increase any stress or tension that you are feeling. It may also disturb your ability to concentrate.

Take at least two HB pencils, a rubber, and a pencil sharpener.

You may not take an English dictionary into the exam. Bilingual students may get special permission from the awarding body to take a small dictionary that translates their home language into English.

You must find out what the local regulations are with regard to taking refreshments into the exam. If you are allowed refreshments, be considerate to others and do not take anything that rustles or makes a noise.

Times and dates

Make sure that you know the exact time and date of the exam and where it will be held. If you miss this sitting, you will have to wait a few months before the next examination.

Other information

Remember that the exam is designed to test your knowledge and understanding and not to trick or mislead you.

The majority of candidates pass the exam, but if you do not, do not despair. Ask for help to prepare well for the next sitting. Currently there are three a year. Very occasionally a student unexpectedly fails. This can be very distressing, especially if they have been successful in completing every other part of the course. If this happens to you, discuss it with your tutor who will decide whether to contact the awarding body on your behalf.

It is always encouraging when people wish you good luck for an exam and the authors of this book wish you every success. But remember that the key to success is not luck – it is preparation!

7 SAMPLE MCQ PAPERS

PAPER 1 *(Answers on page 208)*

1   The most important reason for immunising children is to prevent:
   a)   Side-effects of the disease
   b)   Absence from school
   c)   Spread of the disease
   d)   The disease occurring

2   An adult can BEST prevent children's accidents at home by providing:

a) Coiled kettle flex	Window locks	Regular safety checks	Non-slip rugs
b) Constant adult supervision	Stair gate	Fire guard	Locked medicine cupboards
c) Fire guard	Door locks	Socket covers	Cooker guard
d) Window locks	Fire guard	Coiled kettle flex	Socket covers

3   Nursery staff would suspect a 2 year old child is being abused if the child has:

   1   frequent facial bruising
   2   frequent bruising on the abdomen
   3   signs of insecurity with strangers
   4   a short concentration span while playing
   5   frequent bruising on the shins
   6   unexplained absences from nursery

   a)   1, 2, 6
   b)   1, 3, 4
   c)   2, 3, 5
   d)   4, 5, 6

4   When choosing the destination for an outing with children, the child care and education worker should ensure that the venue will be:

a) Within walking distance
b) Appropriate for the age of the children
c) An exciting experience for the children
d) Able to provide adult assistance

5   The MAIN benefits of outdoor play for children are:

1   The opportunity to share and take turns
2   Helping obese children to burn calories
3   Helping development of the lungs
4   Children are less boisterous after playing outside
5   Improving co-ordination and muscle tone
6   Helping the digestion of food

a) 1, 2, 4, 6
b) 1, 3, 5, 6
c) 3, 4, 5, 6
d) 1, 2, 3, 5

6   James can ride a tricycle using the pedals, kick a ball hard, climb a ladder to nursery slide, stand and walk on tiptoe and walk upstairs with one foot to a step. James is aged:

a) 2 years
b) 18 months
c) 2 years and six months
d) 3 years

7   When playing with bricks, most children aged 18 months can build:

a) Steps with six bricks
b) A tower of three bricks
c) A tower of six bricks
d) A bridge with three bricks

8   Dental health can BEST be improved by

1   Regular dental checks
2   Using fluoride toothpaste
3   Cleaning teeth after meals
4   Using fluoride tablets
5   Reducing carbohydrate in the diet
6   Cutting out snacks between meals

a) 1, 2, 3, 4
b) 1, 2, 3, 6
c) 1, 3, 5, 6
d) 3, 4, 5, 6

9 Carbohydrate is necessary in the diet because it:

a) Provides material for growth
b) Helps to form haemoglobin
c) Provides heat and energy
d) Is essential for bone formation

10 Insufficient vitamin D in the diet may cause:

a) Poor night vision
b) Rickets
c) Scurvy
d) Delayed blood clotting

11 To help a family on a limited budget to plan a balanced diet, a child care worker must know:

a) Which shops have special offers
b) Which cheaper foods contain essential nutrients
c) Where to buy foods in bulk
d) How to prepare and cook cheaper foods

12 A child with Coeliac disease must restrict intake of:

a) Glucose
b) Gluten
c) Protein
d) Sugar

13 A normal temperature is:

a) 35°c
b) 36°c
c) 37°c
d) 38°c

14 In case of an asthma attack, a child's inhaler should be:

a) Kept in the child's school bag
b) In the teacher's desk drawer
c) Immediately available to the child
d) In the classroom First Aid box

15 Displays are MOST important for children because they:

    1   Show adults' work
    2   Encourage sensory exploration
    3   Increase self-esteem
    4   Decorate the environment
    5   Increase knowledge
    6   Promote discussion

    a) 1, 2, 3, 4
    b) 2, 3, 5, 6
    c) 2, 3, 4, 5
    d) 3, 4, 5, 6

16 Play is of MOST value to children when it:

    a) Keeps them occupied
    b) Prevents them from becoming bored
    c) Is a varied learning experience
    d) Stops them behaving unsociably

17 During the Sensory Motor stage of development, adults can BEST support children's learning by providing them with:

    a) The materials and an environment for imaginative role play
    b) Opportunities for discussion and review
    c) Objects to explore and experience
    d) Tools to make calculations and understand concepts

18 Non- verbal communication includes:

a) Body language	Talking	Singing
b) Facial expressions	Gestures	Eye contact
c) Singing	Reading aloud	Speaking
d) Asking questions	Discussion	Gestures

19 A child care and education worker is planning a cooking activity. This activity will PRIMARILY stimulate:

a) All-round development and sensory awareness
b) Fine manipulative skills
c) Intellectual and conceptual skills
d) Gross motor skills

20 Which combination of equipment will best stimulate fine manipulative skills when used by a young child?

a) Water	Dry sand	Dough
b) Jigsaws	Collage activity	Beads and thread
c) Hats	Dolls	Pushchairs
d) Bicycles	Trucks	Tyres

21 Which of the following practices discriminates unfairly?

a) Children not being allowed to go to school when they have an acute infectious illness
b) Children only being allowed to go on an outing if their parents can pay for it
c) Children only being allowed to play out in winter if their coats are fastened
d) Children not being allowed to go swimming if they have a bad cold

22 Promoting equality of opportunity in a school includes:

a) Treating everyone the same
b) Ignoring the differences that exist between children
c) Providing the same facilities for all children
d) Recognising differences and enabling all children to participate

23 A THEORY of social and emotional development is:

a) An idea about why children develop in the way that they do
b) A list of stages of development
c) An indication of the ages at which development occurs
d) A comparison of different ages of development

24 By what age can children normally first distinguish between different family members and act socially with them?

   a) 1 year
   b) 18 months
   c) 2 years
   d) 2 years and 6 months

25 A 3-year-old child is upset when her parent leaves her at her new day nursery to go to work for the day. The best thing the child care and education worker can do is to:

   a) Tell the child to be brave and go and play because her parent won't be long
   b) Tell her to concentrate on playing with some new jigsaws
   c) Stay with the child and play with her while she settles
   d) Encourage her to go and play with a group of more settled children

26 Which of the following, if said by a young child, would enable you to assess that the child had high self-esteem?

   a) "I can't do that – I'm no good at painting"
   b) "Will you help me to tie my laces?"
   c) "I'm good at doing up my buttons."
   d) "Is it my turn to go on a bike?"

27 Children usually develop a mature level of self-discipline:

   a) By their first birthday
   b) As soon as they can walk
   c) Gradually during childhood
   d) When they start school

28 In reaction to a stranger, a child of one year is most likely to:

   a) Be shy and cling to their carer
   b) Be happy as long as the stranger is kind
   c) Not mind being with the stranger
   d) Show positive interest in the stranger

29 The term 'normal behaviour' best describes:

   a) The age-appropriate behaviour of a child
   b) The behaviour of a child at school
   c) Any behaviour that is acceptable at home
   d) Behaviour that is very mature for the age of the child

30 The management of children's behaviour through Behaviour Modification techniques emphasises:

    a) Promoting and rewarding positive aspects of children's behaviour
    b) Punishing each instance of negative behaviour
    c) Paying close attention to children when they behave negatively
    d) Rewarding both positive and negative behaviour equally

31 Between which years are children characteristically possessive and more prone to extreme swings of mood and behaviour?

    a) 1 and 2 years
    b) 2 and 3 years
    c) 3 and 4 years
    d) 4 and 5 years

32 To work successfully with children and their parents/carers, child care workers should acknowledge that parents:

    1 Are the main educators of their children
    2 Know and understand their children
    3 Need to be told how to care for their children
    4 Prefer to leave educating their children to professionals
    5 Will value being involved in the education of their children
    6 Can share knowledge with staff to benefit their children

    a) 1, 3, 4, 6
    b) 1, 2, 5, 6
    c) 2, 4, 5, 6
    d) 3, 4, 5, 6

33 The legislation that led to the formation of the Welfare State was introduced during the:

    a) 1930s
    b) 1940s
    c) 1950s
    d) 1960s

34 The statutory age at which children must receive full time education is:

    a) From the day after their fifth birthday
    b) At the beginning of the term in which they are five
    c) From the beginning of the year in which they are five
    d) At the beginning of the term after their fifth birthday

35 A 'means-tested' benefit from the government is one that:

    a) Only people whose income is below a certain level can receive

    b) Only people who have families can receive

    c) All people can receive whatever their income

    d) Only people who are in full-time work can receive

36 Which of the following is NOT a voluntary organisation?

    a) RELATE

    b) NSPCC

    c) DSS

    d) NCH

37 The best way to discourage headlice is to:

    a) Shampoo the hair daily

    b) Use a special shampoo

    c) Comb the hair regularly

    d) Keep the hair short

38 Which of the following are the MOST useful in encouraging energetic outdoor exercise for children aged 4–7 years?

    1   Skipping ropes

    2   Tricycles and bicycles

    3   Prams and trolleys

    4   Balls

    5   Hoops

    6   Trucks

    a) 1, 2, 3

    b) 1, 2, 4

    c) 3, 4, 5

    d) 4, 5, 6

39 Examples of parasites which infest humans are:

    1   Headlice

    2   Ringworm

    3   Impetigo

    4   Scabies

    5   Seborrhoea

    6   Threadworm

a) 1, 2, 3, 5
b) 1, 2, 4, 6
c) 2, 3, 4, 6
d) 3, 4, 5, 6

40 To ensure access to a nursery unit for a child using a wheelchair, there should be:

1   Access to resources
2   Enough space between furniture
3   Changing facilities
4   Wide doorways
5   Special needs assistance
6   Ramps

a) 1, 2, 3
b) 1, 4, 6
c) 2, 3, 5
d) 2, 4, 6

PAPER 2 *(Answers on page 208)*

1 Children are very vulnerable to infection because they:

    a) Do not wash their hands properly
    b) Play outside
    c) Have immature immune systems
    d) Have not been immunised

2 Workplace safety policies and procedures are important because they:

    a) Reassure parents and carers
    b) Provide a planned programme of accident prevention
    c) Encourage children to behave in a sensible and responsible manner
    d) Make it clear to children and staff what is expected of them

3 A child in your care scalds themselves with a hot cup of tea. The correct First Aid treatment is to:

    a) Rub it with butter
    b) Cover with a dry lint-free dressing
    c) Immerse in tepid water for 10 minutes
    d) Immerse in cold water for 10 minutes

4 If a child care worker in an Infant school suspects abuse s/he should report this to the:

    a) Health Visitor
    b) Class teacher
    c) Social worker
    d) Designated teacher

5 When planning an outing, the MOST IMPORTANT considerations are:

    1 The cost of transport
    2 Choosing a destination
    3 Parental consent
    4 First Aid kit
    5 Taking spare clothes
    6 Adequate adult/child ratios

    a) 1, 2, 3
    b) 1, 3, 5
    c) 2, 3, 6
    d) 4, 5, 6

6   Gross motor skills can best be stimulated by:

a)   Threading beads
b)   Riding a tricycle
c)   Catching balls
d)   Building with bricks

7   At 18 months most children are able to:

1   Walk alone
2   Run without falling
3   Squat to pick up toys
4   Walk upstairs with hand(s) held
5   Ride a tricycle using pedals
6   Stand on tiptoe

a)   1, 2, 3
b)   1, 3, 4
c)   1, 5, 6
d)   2, 4, 5

8   Most children will be able to tie their own shoelaces by the age of:

a)   3
b)   4
c)   5
d)   6

9   In choosing children's clothing the most important considerations are:

1   Colour
2   Washability
3   Fashion
4   Comfort
5   Warmth
6   Easy fastening

a)   1, 2, 3, 4
b)   1, 3, 4, 5
c)   2, 3, 5, 6
d)   2, 4, 5, 6

10 Successful bowel and bladder control can best be achieved by:

a)   Waiting until the child is ready to be toilet-trained
b)   Offering rewards for using the potty
c)   Taking the child to the toilet every hour
d)   Showing displeasure when accidents occur

11 Complete proteins supply:

    a)   5 essential amino acids

    b)   10 essential amino acids

    c)   8 essential amino acids

    d)   9 essential amino acids

12 Which vitamin CANNOT be stored by the body?

    a)   A

    b)   C

    c)   D

    d)   K

13 Which foods could be eaten by a child following a Vegan diet?

    a)   Vegetable omelette

    b)   Cheese sandwich

    c)   Fish pie

    d)   Baked beans

14 Raw meat and fish should be stored:

    a)   On the top shelf of a refrigerator

    b)   In a container in the kitchen

    c)   On the bottom shelf of a refrigerator

    d)   Wrapped in a cool place

15 A child with chickenpox will have:

    a)   Flat blotchy rash

    b)   Blistering spots and scabs

    c)   Koplik's spots

    d)   Fine pinhead spots

16 Encouraging ill children to drink frequently is important because drinking will:

    a)   Replace food intake

    b)   Prevent dehydration

    c)   Wash out the system

    d)   Stimulate the appetite

17 The class is late for dinner because of a concert rehearsal. John has diabetes and is feeling unwell. The child care worker should:

a) Check that John has had his insulin
b) Give John a glucose drink
c) Get John into dinner quickly
d) Sit John down some where quiet

18 A 2-year-old child comes to the day nursery with a comfort blanket. The BEST response from the child care and education worker is to:

a) Encourage the parent/carer to take the blanket home
b) Explain to the child that they will be too busy to need it
c) Keep the blanket in the staff room in case it is needed
d) Allow the child to keep the blanket with them

19 Play is described as 'parallel' when a child plays:

a) Alone with toys and other materials
b) Alongside another child without interacting
c) At the same activity, sometimes communicating with another child
d) Interactively with a group of children

20 BEST use will be made of materials for creative and imaginative play by:

1 Providing cupboards to keep them safely out of children's reach
2 Adults putting things away neatly and tidily
3 Clear labelling of containers for different materials
4 Children being able to use them independently
5 Storing things at children's height
6 Adults getting materials out in an orderly way

a) 1, 2, 3
b) 1, 4, 6
c) 2, 5, 6
d) 3, 4, 5

21 Which of the following activities is MOST likely to encourage communication skills in a 3-year-old?

a) A variety of jigsaw puzzles
b) Attractive construction toys
c) A varied messy play area
d) Discussion and review time

22 The primary value of role play for the young child is that it stimulates:

    a) Gross and fine motor skills
    b) Imaginative and imitative skills
    c) Intellectual and conceptual skills
    d) Sensory development

23 A child in the nursery develops sickness and diarrhoea. What should the child care worker do FIRST?

    a) Call for the doctor
    b) Tell the supervisor
    c) Send for the parent
    d) Comfort and reassure the child

24 Which combination of equipment will best stimulate gross manipulative skills when used by a young child?

a)	Balls	Hoops	Bats
b)	Jigsaws	Collage activity	Beads and thread
c)	Hats	Dolls	Small bricks
d)	Bicycles	Trucks	Climbing frame

25 Which of the following children are LEAST likely to experience the effects of negative stereotypical assumptions?

    a) White able-bodied children
    b) Children from black and other minority ethnic groups
    c) Children with physical impairments
    d) Girls from any background

26 The Children Act 1989 defined the services that should be provided by a Local Authority for:

    a) All children in the area
    b) Children in need in that area
    c) Only children under 5 in that area
    d) Only children of statutory school age in the area

27 A biological theory of development is based on the idea that children:

a) Are born with a genetic make-up that determines how they respond and behave
b) Are born with a set of needs that must be met for healthy development
c) Develop because of the experiences and contact they have with other people
d) Develop as they do because of what they learn in childhood

28 By what age do children first begin to follow their carer around, and imitate them by helping with small household tasks?

a) 1 year
b) 18 months
c) 2 years
d) 2 years and 6 months

29 A 'transition period' in a child's life refers to the:

a) Time a child has spent in a nursery
b) Movement of a child from one place of care to another
c) Period that a child has spent in a school
d) The years between 3 and 4

30 A nursery worker who is trying to encourage self-help skills in young children will be more successful if s/he says:

a) "Come on, you can do it yourself. You are a big boy/girl now."
b) "That's clever! Shall I help you with this bit if you cannot manage?"
c) "You'll have a present if you do it all by yourself."
d) "Look – everyone else has done it. You can do it too."

31 Child care and education workers are MOST likely to have realistic expectations of children's behaviour if they:

a) Understand age-appropriate behaviour
b) Read many books
c) Are stricter with children to start with
d) Provide few boundaries for children

32 By what age can a child FIRST be expected to be aware of when it is appropriate to be quiet or noisy?

a) 1 year
b) 2 years
c) 3 years
d) 4 years

33 Children are most likely to develop socially acceptable behaviour patterns if they are:

    1   Given attention whenever they demand it
    2   Given clear boundaries
    3   Have adult attention as they work and play
    4   Told off each time they behave unacceptably
    5   Praised when they behave acceptably
    6   Punished when they are aggressive

    a) 1 ,2 ,4
    b) 1 ,3 ,6
    c) 2 ,3 ,5
    d) 4 ,5 ,6

34 When using Behaviour Modification techniques, the best way to discourage unwanted behaviour is to:

    a) Give the child lots of attention when they behave negatively
    b) Reward the child when they behave negatively
    c) Use physical restraint whenever it is needed
    d) Give the negative behaviour little open attention

35 When settling a child into a new setting, it will be MOST helpful if the child care worker:

    a) Settles the child in gradually
    b) Sends the parents information
    c) Tells the other children about the new child
    d) Makes sure the child's peg is labelled

36 When communicating with parents, it is ESSENTIAL that child care workers ensure that:

    a) Parents receive regular letters
    b) Communication is a two-way process
    c) There is a parents' noticeboard
    d) An information booklet is available

37 STATUTORY services are MAINLY funded from:

    a) Voluntary donations
    b) Taxes and national insurance
    c) Fundraising events
    d) Profits from business

38 Local Authorities in England and Wales:

    a) Must provide nursery education for some children over 4 years old

    b) Must provide nursery education for all children after they are 3 years old

    c) Must provide nursery education for some children after they are 3 years old

    d) Can provide nursery education for all children after they are 3 years old

39 Family Credit is a government benefit that:

    a) A parent who works more than 16 hours for a low wage can receive

    b) All people whose income is low can claim

    c) A person who is unemployed can claim

    d) A parent who works less than 16 hours for a low wage can receive

40 In which year was The Children Act passed by Parliament?

    a) 1986

    b) 1989

    c) 1992

    d) 1997

PAPER 3   (Answers on page 208)

1   The MOST EFFECTIVE methods for preventing the spread of infection in a child care establishment are:

   1   Good ventilation
   2   Cleaning out pet cages regularly
   3   Encouraging children to wash their hands regularly
   4   Using paper towels to dry hands
   5   Excluding children with an infection
   6   Reducing the heating temperature

   a)   1, 2, 4
   b)   1, 3, 5
   c)   2, 3, 5
   d)   4, 5, 6

2   Child care and education workers can BEST help to ensure children's safety at home-time by:

   a)   Encouraging children to remain in the building for collection
   b)   Providing a crossing patrol
   c)   Only releasing children to a known adult
   d)   Producing a written procedure for collecting children

3   If a child care and education worker finds an unconscious child, their FIRST action should be to:

   a)   Send for the headteacher
   b)   Check for breathing
   c)   Send for an ambulance
   d)   Contact the parents

4   An emotional indicator of abuse is:

   a)   Burns
   b)   Inappropriate behaviour
   c)   Inappropriate clothing
   d)   Repeated accidental injuries

5   A safe adult/child ratio for 2–5-year-old children on an outing is:

   a)   1 adult to 2 children
   b)   1 adult to 3 children
   c)   1 adult to 4 children
   d)   2 adults to 5 children

6 To develop confidence and co-ordination in gross motor skills, children should be offered the opportunity to:

1 Practise new skills
2 Socialise with other children
3 Learn from experience
4 Play team games
5 Play outdoors with supervision
6 Explore new environments

a) 1, 2, 3, 4
b) 1, 3, 5, 6
c) 2, 3, 4, 6
d) 3, 4, 5, 6

7 To learn to walk unaided, children need:

1 A baby walker
2 Stable furniture
3 Head control
4 Well-fitting shoes
5 Opportunity to practise
6 An encouraging adult

a) 1, 2, 3, 4
b) 1, 2, 4, 6
c) 2, 3, 5, 6
d) 3, 4, 5, 6

8 A child aged 3 years should be able to:

a) Build three steps with six bricks	Thread small beads	Copy a square
b) Build a tower of 9/10 small bricks	Cut with scissors	Copy a circle
c) Catch a ball	Draw recognisable pictures	Thread a needle
d) Draw a diamond shape	Sew neatly with needle and thread	Tie shoelaces

9 Children's shoes should:

    1   Protect the feet without rubbing or chaffing the skin
    2   Be flexible and allow free movement
    3   Be cleaned regularly
    4   Have room for growth
    5   Be changed every three months
    6   Have an adjustable fastener

    a) 1, 2, 3, 4
    b) 1, 2, 4, 6
    c) 2, 3, 5, 6
    d) 3, 4, 5, 6

10 Fat is essential in the diet because it:

    1   Provides energy
    2   Stores vitamins
    3   Strengthens bones
    4   Makes food palatable
    5   Helps growth
    6   Contains vitamin C

    a) 1, 3, 4, 6
    b) 1, 2, 3, 4
    c) 2, 4, 5, 6
    d) 3, 4, 5, 6

11 Which vitamin helps the absorption of iron?

    a) C
    b) D
    c) K
    d) E

12 Pathogens may enter the body through a cut or graze and cause:

    a) Chickenpox
    b) Thrush
    c) Hepatitis
    d) Meningitis

13 'E' numbers label:

    a) Permitted food additives
    b) Sell-by dates
    c) Natural ingredients
    d) Vitamin E content

14 Koplik's spots can be seen in the mouth if a child has:

a) Rubella
b) Chickenpox
c) Scarlet fever
d) Measles

15 Thrush is caused by a:

a) Fungus
b) Parasite
c) Bacteria
d) Virus

16 When caring for a child who is unwell at nursery, the CCE worker should:

1 Provide reassurance
2 Isolate the child
3 Give practical help
4 Keep the child company
5 Relax their expectations
6 Provide challenging play

a) 1, 2, 4, 5
b) 1, 3, 4, 5
c) 2, 3, 5, 6
d) 2, 3, 4, 6

17 A child who has Coeliac disease should NOT eat food containing:

a) Glucose
b) Gluten
c) Protein
d) Carbohydrate

18 During a story session with a group of 3–4-year-olds the window cleaner starts to clean the classroom windows. The child care worker should:

a) Move to another room
b) Try to keep the children's attention on the story
c) Ask the window cleaner to stop until after the story
d) Begin a discussion about cleaning windows

19 Play is described as 'solitary' when a child plays:

a) Alone with toys
b) Alongside another child without interacting
c) At the same activity and communicates with another child
d) Interactively with a group of children

20 The MOST important aspects of the adult role when providing play for young children are:

1 Participating appropriately
2 Planning activities
3 Producing good results
4 Preventing damage
5 Putting things away
6 Preparing materials
7 Preventing disruption
8 Providing opportunities

a) 1, 2, 6, 8
b) 1, 2, 5, 7
c) 3, 4, 5, 7
d) 3, 4, 6, 8

21 In a school where there are children whose home language is not that of the dominant group, it is now considered to be good practice to:

1 Provide all books in the dominant language to encourage familiarity
2 Encourage home languages while providing support in the dominant language
3 Encourage the use of the dominant language whenever possible
4 Value language diversity through materials and usage
5 Promote home languages through the use of displays, books and signs
6 Discourage home language use in school

a) 1, 2, 6
b) 1, 3, 6
c) 2, 4, 5
d) 3, 4, 5

22 Tabletop games are of great value in helping children to arrange things in a particular order. This skill is sometimes referred to as:

a) Matching
b) Conceptualising
c) Concentrating
d) Sequencing

23 The MAIN benefits of providing musical activities for young children are to promote:

a) Spatial awareness	Emotional development	Listening skills
b) Emotional development	Sequencing skills	Fine motor skills
c) Social development	Fine motor skills	Spatial awareness
d) Sequencing skills	Social development	Listening skills

24 Which combination of equipment will best stimulate gross motor skills when used by a young child?

a) Balls	Hoops	Bats
b) Jigsaws	Collage activity	Beads and thread
c) Hats	Dolls	Small bricks
d) Bicycles	Trucks	Climbing frame

25 Research shows that women in employment:
a) Are now as successful as men in any workplace
b) Are in the majority in high status jobs
c) Are more often employed in low status jobs
d) Experience no discrimination at work

26 Many employers have a code of practice concerning equal opportunities. The most important aspect of this is that it makes clear statements about:
a) The pay structure of the organisation
b) The amount of holiday each employees is entitled to
c) The treatment of employees within the organisation
d) The policy towards early retirement

27 Within an infant school, the things that will BEST enable all children to feel valued are:

1 Having regular assemblies
2 Providing a variety of positive images of children in books
3 Having class sizes below 30 children
4 Having displays that reflect a multi-ethnic, multi-ability society
5 Recognising each child's individual needs
6 Holding regular staff meetings

a) 1, 2, 3
b) 1, 4, 6
c) 2, 4, 5
d) 3, 5, 6

28 A 'social learning' theory of development is based on the idea that children:

a) Are born with a genetic make-up that determines how they respond and behave
b) Are born with needs that must be met for healthy development
c) Develop because they observe and have contact with other people
d) Develop as they do because of what they inherit from their parents

29 By what age can children consistently demonstrate that they have control of their emotions, self-containment and independence?

a) 1 year
b) 3 years
c) 5 years
d) 7 years

30 When separated from its main carer, a 2-year-old child will benefit MOST from nursery care that includes:

a) A large, lively, stimulating group of young children
b) A set routine that is applied to the children in the nursery
c) A group of children of a wide variety of ages
d) A key worker system that has a high ratio of carers to children

31 A young child is upset and tells you that her pet cat died at the weekend. The BEST way to help the child would be to:

a) Offer her a stimulating activity that morning
b) Tell her about when your cat died
c) Encourage her to play with a lively group of children
d) Listen and let her talk to you

32 The 'antecedent' to a child's behaviour is:

  a) What happens afterwards
  b) What the child actually does
  c) The acceptable parts of the behaviour
  d) What happened before the behaviour occurred

33 At what age are children MOST likely to be possessive of toys and have little concept of sharing?

  a) 1 year
  b) 2 years
  c) 3 years
  d) 4 years

34 Norms of behaviour are:

  a) The beliefs that behaviour is based on
  b) Behaviour that is unacceptable to a group
  c) The personal attitudes of an individual
  d) The rules and customs about actual behaviour

35 Frequent episodes of difficult and challenging behaviour are more likely to occur because a child:

  1 Has learned they only get attention if they misbehave
  2 Is seeking attention
  3 Has usually been rewarded for behaving well
  4 Has had too much attention when behaving positively

  a) 1, 2
  b) 1, 3
  c) 2, 4
  d) 3, 4

36 In a situation where there is conflict with parents, a child care worker should:

  a) Tell the parents that professionals know best
  b) Take parents' concerns seriously
  c) Explain to the parents why they are wrong
  d) Make a note of any complaints

37 Any written records about children and their carers should be:

  a) Freely available to all the staff
  b) Kept in the office to which only staff have access
  c) Stored securely and confidentiality maintained
  d) Available to the head teacher/manager only

38 Which of the following organisations have the main responsibility for providing STATUTORY services?

1 Private organisations
2 Local voluntary groups
3 Local government departments
4 Self-help groups
5 Business and industry
6 National voluntary organisations
7 The National Lottery Board
8 Central government departments

a) 1, 5
b) 2, 6
c) 4, 7
d) 3, 8

39 The political framework for the provision of services in Britain is democratic. This means that decisions about what services will be provided are made by:

a) Politicians who are voted into office by citizens
b) Members of the armed forces
c) One leader who rules the country
d) A self-appointed committee

40 The commonest cause of death amongst toddlers and young children is

a) Child abuse
b) Accidents
c) Infections
d) Cancers

APPENDIX A
NVQ Knowledge Evidence checklists

> **This Appendix covers:**
> - How to use the Knowledge Evidence Charts
> - Knowledge Evidence Tasks for the core units Child Care and Education at Level 2

While you are working towards your NVQ award you will be required by your assessor to demonstrate your practical competence. **In addition to this, your assessor will also need to have evidence that you have sufficient knowledge and understanding to complement your practical skills.** Your assessor may be able to judge and assess this through your performance evidence, but you will also need to provide other evidence in addition or to support this.

The knowledge evidence required for each element is specified in the candidate's book. For example:

Knowledge Evidence
Evidence of an appropriate level of knowledge and understanding in the following areas is required to be demonstrated from the above assessment process, supplemented as necessary from oral or written questions or other knowledge tests or from evidence of prior learning.

C.2.1.a The nutritional value of common foodstuffs and drinks and what constitutes a balanced diet
C.2.1.b The nutritional value in relation to size of portions and methods of preparation
C.2.1.c Ways of presenting food and drink that are attractive to children and easy to manage.
C.2.1.d Health and safety requirements in relation to food preparation and storage.
C.2.1.e Common dietary requirements associated with religious and cultural practices.

How to use the Knowledge Evidence Charts

On the following pages you will find charts which contain tasks related to the Knowledge Evidence for each core unit and element for the NVQ Child Care and Education award at Level 2.

Each chart shows you:

- The unit and element of the award
- The task you need to do to provide evidence of your knowledge
- A reference to the 'spreads' found earlier in this book, so that you can find information to help you complete the tasks
- A box to tick when you have completed the tasks so that you can keep a record of your progress

The charts appear in the following order:

- C2: Care for children's physical needs
- C4: Support for children's social and emotional development
- C6: Contribute to the management of children's behaviour
- C8: Set out and clear away play activities
- C9: Work with young children
- E1: Maintain a child-oriented environment
- E2: Maintain the safety of children
- P2: Establish and maintain relationships with parents of young children

NVQ UNIT C2

Care for children's physical needs

Element C2.1: Provide food and drinks for children

ELEMENT	TASK	REFER TO SPREAD	TASK DONE
C2.1a	Read Spreads 13 and 14 and answer the questions at the end of each.	13, 14	☐
C2.1a, b, c	Devise menus for five days for: a) A child aged 3 years b) A child aged 6 years Show the food values and how you have provided a balanced diet. c) Explain how you would present one of the meals to make it attractive to the children.	13, 14, 15	☐
C2.1d	Explain how you would store cooked and fresh food in: a) The fridge b) The freezer c) The kitchen	16	☐
C2.1e	Make a chart showing the different cultural and religious principles relating to diet.	15	☐
C2.1g	Explain why it is important for you and the children to know about these principles.	15	☐
C2.1h	Give examples of the food preferences of a child of 3 years. How do you think these might change by the time the child is 8?	13, 14, 15	☐
C2.1i, j	Make a list of all the common food allergies. For each item say how you would need to adjust the child's diet.	16	☐

NVQ UNIT C2

Care for children's physical needs

Element C2.2: Contribute to children's personal hygiene

ELEMENT	TASK	REFER TO SPREAD	TASK DONE
C2.2a, b	Why is good hygiene important when caring for children? Describe three personal hygiene routines. Say what toiletries and materials will be needed.	1, 11	☐
C2.2c	List five ways in which infection can be spread. What measures can be taken to prevent infection spreading in a child care setting?	1, 17	☐
C2.2d	Describe how you would clean up a blood spill. Why is it important to clean up blood spills carefully?	1	☐
C2.2e	Why do the ways in which we care for the personal hygiene of children vary?	11	☐
C2.2f	Describe the stages of toilet training.	12	☐
C2.2g	a) What are the general signs of infection? b) How do you know a graze is infected? c) What might you notice about a child's stools and urine that would give you cause for concern?	17	☐

NVQ UNIT C2

Care for children's physical needs

Element C2.3: Respond to illness in a child

ELEMENT	TASK	REFER TO SPREAD	TASK DONE
C2.3a, b, c	Read Spreads 17,18,19 and 20 and answer the questions.	17, 18, 19, 20	☐
C2.3b	At what age are general symptoms of illness more worrying?	17	☐
C2.3c	Why is it important to keep records about a child's illnesses?	20	☐
C2.3d	If you were worried about a child's illness when they were in your care, whom would you need to contact? How do you make sure that you can contact these people?	20	☐
C2.3f	A child is unconscious. What are your FIRST actions?	3 ,4	☐
C2.3g	How do varying skin tones affect the appearance of rashes and other signs of illness shown on the skin?	11	☐
C2.3h	If a child is unwell, what changes might you expect in their behaviour during and after the illness?	20	☐
C2.3i	Describe how you would store and label medicines in the home and the nursery. Why is it important to store and label medicines properly?	20	☐

Continued on page 162

Element C2.3 (Contd.)

ELEMENT	TASK	REFER TO SPREAD	TASK DONE
C2.3j	Read Spread 19 and answer the questions.	19	☐
C2.3k	A child in your care has a condition needing long-term care. What help and support will the parents need?	35	☐
C2.3l	Read Spread 20 and answer the questions.	20	☐

NVQ UNIT C2

Care for children's physical needs

Element C2.4: Provide opportunities for rest and sleep

ELEMENT	TASK	REFER TO SPREAD	TASK DONE
C2,4a	a) Why is it important to have quiet periods of rest/sleep as a regular part of each child's day? b) Why is it important to keep to a young child's routine of rest /sleep? c) How can a nursery caring for a babies and young children ensure that this happens?	11	☐
C2.4b	Record the rest and sleep patterns of a 2-year-old and a 4-year-old over 24 hours. Note and compare the differences.	11	☐

C2.4c, d	Describe how you would provide areas for quiet/rest/sleep in:
	   a) A nursery for children under 3 years old
	   b) A nursery for children 3–5 years old
	   c) A classroom for children 5–7 years old
	How would you encourage the children to keep these areas for quiet activities?
		11, 21	☐

C2.4e	Describe and compare two different approaches to bedtime.	11	☐
C2.4f	Describe the problems some families might have about bedtimes	11, 40	☐

NVQ UNIT C2

Care for children's physical needs

Element C2.5: Provide opportunities for children's exercise

ELEMENT	TASK	REFER TO SPREAD	TASK DONE
C2.5a	How does exercise promote: a) Growth? b) Development?	7, 9	☐
C2.5b	Why is it important to supervise children's exercise?	7, 9	☐
C2.5c	Describe two examples of how physical growth relates to physical development.	7, 8, 9, 10	☐
C2.5d	Describe an activity using large equipment for physical exercise. What safety checks and precautions would you need to make when setting up the activity?	9	☐
C2.5e	What type of exercise would you provide to promote: a) Balance? b) Co-ordination? c) Muscle development of the legs? d) Muscle development of the arms? e) Eye-hand co-ordination? f) Self-confidence? g) The circulation of the blood?	7, 8, 9, 10	☐

NVQ UNIT C4

Support children's social and emotional development

Element C4.1: Help children relate to others

ELEMENT	TASK	REFER TO SPREAD	TASK DONE
C4.1a	How can child care workers encourage children to relate to others? What activities can be provided to encourage this?	36	☐
C4.1b	What is the role of the child care worker in helping children resolve conflicts? Explain and give reasons for your answers.	36, 39	☐
C4.1c	What is a role model? Describe how adults can act as role models for children who are learning to relate to others.	32, 36, 39	☐

NVQ UNIT C4

Support children's social and emotional development

Element C4.2: Help children to develop self-reliance and self-esteem

ELEMENT	TASK	REFER TO SPREAD	TASK DONE
C4.2	Write a short paragraph to describe and define: a) Self-reliance b) Self-esteem c) Self-image	33, 34, 35, 36	☐
C4.2a, h	Describe activities which will encourage self-reliance or self-esteem in a child aged: a) 1–2 years b) 3–5 years c) 5–7 years	36	☐
C4.2b	Why is it important for adults working with children to have self-respect?	36	☐
C4.2c	Describe the stages in the development of independence and how this is influenced by other areas of development.	12, 33, 34, 36	☐
C4.2d	Why is it important to listen to children? How can the child care worker encourage interaction between children and adults?	23, 36	☐
C4.2e	Describe an example of how you could give some responsibility to a child aged: a) 1–2 years b) 3 years c) 4–5 years d) 5-6 years e) 6–7 years	21, 36	☐

Element C4.2 (Contd.)

ELEMENT	TASK	REFER TO SPREAD	TASK DONE
C4.2f	Why is it important to praise children for their efforts?	36, 40	☐
C4.2g	How can adults encourage children to negotiate with each other?	36	☐
C4.2	How can the child care worker interact with parents to reinforce a child's positive self-image and esteem? Why is it important to do this?	36, 37	☐

NVQ UNIT C4

Support children's social and emotional development

Element C4.3: Help children to recognise and deal with their feelings

ELEMENT	TASK	REFER TO SPREAD	TASK DONE
C4.3a	What social and environmental factors could have a negative affect on children's emotional and social development?	35, 36, 37	☐
C4.3b, c, d	Give some examples of: a) Positive emotions/feelings b) Negative emotions/feelings Why is it important for children to recognise these feelings? Why is it important for children to learn to deal with these feelings?	33, 34, 36	☐
C4.3e	Give some examples of how an adult can encourage children to express positive and negative feelings.	36, 37, 40	☐
C4.3f	What gender/cultural stereotypes may be attached to expressing feelings/emotions? How can the child care worker avoid reinforcing these?	32, 36	☐
C4.3g	What signs might indicate that a child is distressed?	33, 34, 35, 36, 37	☐
C4.3h	What strategies can be used by the child care worker to deal with negative behaviour? Which of these strategies will lead to a positive outcome?	39, 40	☐
C4.3i	Why is it important to have a calm and reassuring manner when helping children who are upset?	39, 40	☐

Element C4.3 (Contd.)

ELEMENT	TASK	REFER TO SPREAD	TASK DONE
C4.3j	What learning opportunities/activities which are part of the daily routine can help children to express their feelings? How can these be used to help children discuss and control their feelings?	5, 36, 39, 40	☐
C4.3k	What is the role of the child care worker when there are concerns about a child's social and emotional development? Comment on: a) Confidentiality b) Sharing information with parents, colleagues, and other professionals	5, 40	☐

NVQ UNIT C4

Support children's social and emotional development

Element C4.4: Prepare children for moving on to new settings

ELEMENT	TASK	REFER TO SPREAD	TASK DONE
C4.4a	A child has to move to a new child care setting. Describe the needs of the child. Why is it important to plan for and manage the change?	23, 35	☐
C4.4b	Make a list of all the kinds of child care provision available in your area.	43, 44, 46	☐
C4,4c	What would you expect the effects of separation to be on a child aged: a) 1 year b) 2 years c) 4 years d) 6 years	33, 34, 35	☐
C4.4d, e, f, g, h	Describe how a child care worker would prepare a child aged: a) 3 years, moving from a child-minder to a full-time nursery b) 5 years, going from playgroup to full-time school What would be the needs of each child? How could the change be managed effectively? How can the parents be involved? What would be the role of the carer in the old/new settings?	33, 34, 35	☐

NVQ UNIT C4

Support children's social and emotional development

Element C4.5: Help children adjust to the care/education setting

ELEMENT	TASK	REFER TO SPREAD	TASK DONE
C4.5a	Describe the needs of a child new to a care/education setting. How might these needs vary with the age of the child and the child's previous experiences of change and separation?	33, 34, 35	☐
C4.5b	What might the likely effects of change be on the child? Why is sympathetic handling important?	35, 37	☐
C4.5c	Why are comfort objects and familiar routines and activities important?	23	☐
C4.5d, e, f, g, h	Explain the importance of the following factors/strategies when helping children to adjust to the care/education setting: ● Method of welcoming children ● Settling-in policies ● Children's individual needs ● Preparing the other children ● Involving parents	21, 23, 35, 41	☐

NVQ UNIT C6

Contribute to the management of children's behaviour

Element C6.1: Contribute to a framework for children's behaviour

ELEMENT	TASK	REFER TO SPREAD	TASK DONE
C6.1a	When developing a framework for children's behaviour, describe/define: a) Goals b) Boundaries c) Values What factors may limit children's ability to comply with set goals and boundaries?	37, 39	☐
C6.1b	Why is it important to develop a framework for children's behaviour?	39	☐

NVQ UNIT C6

Contribute to the management of children's behaviour

Element C6.2: Promote positive aspects of children's behaviour

ELEMENT	TASK	REFER TO SPREAD	TASK DONE
C6.2a	What is behaviour? What is socially acceptable behaviour, and why might this idea of behaviour vary? Describe how acceptable behaviour is acquired and the influences on its development.	37, 38	☐
C6.2b	Describe the steps involved in Behaviour Modification.	40	☐
C6.2c	Why is it important to explain and discuss acceptable and unwanted behaviour with children?	40	☐

NVQ UNIT C6

Contribute to the management of children's behaviour

Element C6.3: Manage unwanted aspects of children's behaviour

ELEMENT	TASK	REFER TO SPREAD	TASK DONE
C6.3a	Give four examples of unwanted behaviour. For each example say what might provoke the behaviour.	40	☐
C6.3b	Why is it important to deal calmly with unwanted behaviour? Why should physical punishment NOT be used to manage unwanted behaviour?	40	☐
C6.3c	Describe the basic principles of Behaviour Modification.	40	☐
C6.3d	Why is it important to have clearly defined goals and boundaries consistently applied by adults?	39, 40	☐
C6.3e, f	How can a reward system help promote positive behaviour and discourage unwanted behaviour?	40	☐
C6.3f, g	In what circumstances might physical methods of control be used?	40	☐

NVQ UNIT C8

Set out and clear away play activities

Element C8.1: Set out natural and other materials for creative play

ELEMENT	TASK	REFER TO SPREAD	TASK DONE
C8.1a	Define/describe creative play. What areas of development can be promoted by creative play?	28	☐
C8.1b, c, d, e	Make a list of natural and other materials which can be used in creative play. For each item on your list say: a) How it can be used with children b) What safety issues need to be taken into account when using the materials.	28	☐

NVQ UNIT C8

Set out and clear away play activities

Element C8.2: set up physical play activities with large equipment

ELEMENT	TASK	REFER TO SPREAD	TASK DONE
C8.2b	Describe the benefits, to all areas of children's development, of outdoor play	7, 8, 9, 29	☐
C8.2a, c, d, e, f, g, h	Draw a plan to show how large equipment could be set out for physical play activities. • Describe each piece of equipment and its purpose and value in children's development • Describe the safety procedures which should be carried out • Describe what modifications may need to be made to account for the age of the children and children with special needs.	2, 29	☐

NVQ UNIT C8

Set out and clear away play activities

Element C8.3: Provide opportunities and materials to stimulate role play

ELEMENT	TASK	REFER TO SPREAD	TASK DONE
C8.3a	Define role play. Describe the value of role play in children's development.	24, 27	☐
C8.3b, c	Describe a range of pretend areas and activities. For each activity/area, say how you would set it up and explain how it would be used with the children.	27	☐
C8.3d	Why is it important to use the children's ideas when planning and setting up role play?	27	☐
C8.3e	Give some examples of stereotypes (e.g. gender/cultural) that children might express in role play. Explain how you would counteract this.	27, 30, 32	☐
C8.3f	Make a list of materials that could be used in role play. Identify items which reflect different cultural backgrounds.	27	☐

NVQ UNIT C8

Set out and clear away play activities

Element C8.4: Set out equipment for manipulative play

ELEMENT	TASK	REFER TO SPREAD	TASK DONE
C8.4a	Describe/define: • Fine manipulation • Gross manipulation Give three examples of: • Fine manipulative activities • Gross manipulative activities	10, 24, 29	☐
C8,4b, c, d	Write four activity plans: • To promote fine manipulative skills for children aged 3–4 years • To promote fine manipulative skills for children aged 6–7 years • To promote gross manipulative skills for children aged 3–4 years • To promote gross manipulative skills for children aged 6–7 years One of your plans should be for a child who has the use of one hand.	7, 8, 9, 10, 11, 29	☐

NVQ UNIT C8

Set out and clear away play activities

Element C8.5: Set out a selection of books to interest children

ELEMENT	TASK	REFER TO SPREAD	TASK DONE
C8.5a	Make a list of all the places where children can have access to books.	26	☐
C8.5b, c, d	Select a range of 20 children's books suitable for children aged 0–8 years. • Note the author, title and publisher • Include a brief description of each book, e.g. fact, fiction, reference, picture book, the style of the text, type of illustrations, the language used • Include and comment on books which have positive images and are non-discriminatory.	26, 30, 32	☐
C8.5g	What are the important features of an area where children can use books?	26, 32	☐

NVQ UNIT C8

Set out and clear away play activities

Element C8.6: Clear away activities and store equipment

ELEMENT	TASK	REFER TO SPREAD	TASK DONE
C8.6a	Describe suitable arrangements for storing large and small toys and equipment safely.	21, 25	☐
C8.6b, c, d	Why is it important to encourage children to help in clearing away toys and equipment? What can be done to encourage children to participate in clearing away, and how can you make it easier for them to do this?	25	☐
C8.6e, f	What checks need to be made on toys, materials and equipment to ensure their safe use by the children?	25, 28, 29	☐

NVQ UNIT C9

Work with young children

Element C9.1: Participate with children in a singing music session

ELEMENT	TASK	REFER TO SPREAD	TASK DONE
C9.1a, b, c, d, e, f	Make a collection of songs and musical activities suitable for children across the age range 1–8 years. Describe how you have used the songs and activities with the children. Explain how your activities helped to promote children's learning and development.	26	☐
C9.1g	Choose one of your activities and describe how you could use/ adapt it to encourage a child with hearing impairment to participate.	21, 26	☐

NVQ UNIT C9

Work with young children

Element C9.2: Tell/read a story to young children

ELEMENT	TASK	REFER TO SPREAD	TASK DONE
C9.2a, b, c, f	Make a collection of story plans from books that you have used with children across the age range 1–8 years. Include storybooks, picture books and books in a variety of languages. In each plan say how the story helped to promote the children's learning/development.	24, 25, 26	☐
C9.2d	Why are positive images in books important? List some books for children which include examples of positive images.	24, 25, 26, 32	☐
C9.2, g	Choose one of your story plans and describe how you would use it to enable a child with a visual impairment to participate fully.	21, 24, 25, 26	☐

NVQ UNIT C9

Work with young children

Element C9.3: Set out objects of interest and examine them with children

ELEMENT	TASK	REFER TO SPREAD	TASK DONE
C9.3a, b	Make a list of objects that children could examine, explore and use creatively.	24, 28	☐
C9.3c	What objects can be provided to stimulate sensory areas of development?	24, 28, 29	☐
C9.3d	Describe a range of objects representing different cultural backgrounds that you could provide for children to explore.	28	☐

NVQ UNIT C9

Work with children

Element C9.4: Assist children with a cooking activity

ELEMENT	TASK	REFER TO SPREAD	TASK DONE
C9.1a	What hygiene precautions must be taken when preparing for a cooking activity? Why is it important that hygiene rules are observed during cooking?	1, 2, 16, 27	☐
C9.4b	What are the basic components of a balanced diet?	13, 14, 15, 16	☐
C9.4c, d	Provide examples of recipes that can be used in cooking activities with children. Your examples should include: a) Recipes for use with children of different ages b) Recipes that use different cooking processes	27	☐
C9.4e	Describe how you would adapt a cooking activity so that a child who has difficulty in controlling the movements of one arm might join in.	10, 27, 29	☐
C9.4f	Describe how a cooking activity can promote all-round development.	15, 27, 29	☐

NVQ UNIT C9

Work with children

Element C9.5: Play a game with children

ELEMENT	TASK	REFER TO SPREAD	TASK DONE
C9.5a	What mathematical concepts can be promoted by tabletop games?	25, 27	☐
C9.5b, c, d, j	Make a list of games that could be used to promote children's development. Include examples of: a) Tabletop games b) Physical action games c) Competitive games d) Non-competitive games e) Improvised games	24, 25, 26, 27, 28	☐
C9.5e	How might playing competitive games affect a child's self-esteem?	24, 33, 34, 36	☐
C9.5f	Give examples of how some games might encourage gender stereotyping and say how you would counteract this.	24, 25	☐
C9.5g	What is the expected sequence of development of children's play?	24	☐
C9.5	What strategies can be used to help a child who is reluctant to join in play?	25	☐

NVQ UNIT C9

Work with children

Element C9.6: Participate in a talking and listening activity with children

ELEMENT	TASK	REFER TO SPREAD	TASK DONE
C9.6a	Make a list of games that will encourage children to talk and listen. Explain and justify your choices and say what age the game is suitable for.	27, 28, 29	☐
C9.6b	What are the different types of communication? Name an activity to promote each example given.	26	☐
C9.6c	Describe how the physical layout of a play area can encourage and discourage communication.	21, 25, 26	☐
C9.6d	List some common communication difficulties in young children.	26	☐
C9.6	Describe a talking and listening game. How could you adapt it to enable a child with a hearing impairment to participate?	26	☐

NVQ UNIT C9

Work with children

Element C9.7: Support children's involvement in activities

ELEMENT	TASK	REFER TO SPREAD	TASK DONE
C9.7a, b, c, d	Describe when it is appropriate to interact and intervene in children's play to ensure safety and yet encourage independence and self-esteem.	25	☐
C9.7c	List some health and safety considerations for indoor and outdoor play.	2, 7, 8, 9, 25, 28, 29	☐
C9.7d	Explain why it is important to encourage children to participate in choosing activities and in setting them out and clearing away.	24, 25	☐

NVQ UNIT E1

Maintain a child-oriented environment

Element E1.1: Maintain the physical environment for young children

ELEMENT	TASK	REFER TO SPREAD	TASK DONE
E1.1a	What is the required room temperature in a nursery? Why is good lighting important? Why is it important that exits are not obstructed?	21	☐
E1.1b	What essential instructions should be displayed on a fire notice?	21	☐
E1.1c, d	Draw a plan of a nursery or classroom. Indicate places where children can: a) Work together b) Work alone c) Feel secure Show access points and indicate where modification wiil be needed for children with special needs.	21, 22, 23	☐
E1.1f	What benefits will children get from being able to participate in making decisions about their environment.?	21, 22, 23	☐
E1.1g	Why is it important to provide a safe and secure environment for children? Give some examples of how this will help the child to grow and develop.	21, 22, 23, 1, 2	☐

NVQ UNIT E1

Maintain a child-oriented environment

Element E1.2: Maintain an attractive and stimulating environment for young children

ELEMENT	TASK	REFER TO SPREAD	TASK DONE
E1.2a	What are the features of a good display? Why is it important to display children's work? How can displays help children's learning?	22	☐
E1.2b	Describe three different techniques used for mounting children's work. Describe three different ways in which work can be displayed.	22	☐
E1.2c	What plants and other natural materials can safely be used in displays?	21, 22	☐
E1.2d	Give two examples of plants that might be grown by the children and describe how they would be cared for.	21, 22	☐

NVQ UNIT E1

Maintain a child-oriented environment

Element E1.3: Maintain a reassuring environment for children

ELEMENT	TASK	REFER TO SPREAD	TASK DONE
E1.3a	Give examples of common fears that children might have. Give examples for babies, toddlers, pre-school children and older children.	23, 33, 34, 35	☐
E1 3b, c	How might children show that they are afraid? How might this be different for babies, toddlers, pre-school children and older children? For each of your examples describe how you would deal with the children's fears	23	☐
E1.3d	How can the child care setting provide a reassuring environment for children? Give examples of the equipment and materials needed to do this.	21, 22, 23	☐

NVQ UNIT E2

Maintain the safety of children

Element E2.1: Maintain a safe environment for children

ELEMENT	TASK	REFER TO SPREAD	TASK DONE
E2.1	Why is it important to maintain a hygienic environment when caring for children? Describe the hygiene routines necessary to keep the environment clean and hygienic.	1, 2, 21	☐
E2.2b, f	Why is it important to have routine safety checks for equipment and premises? If problems with equipment occur, what action should be taken? How can you ensure that you set up equipment so that it is safe to use?	2, 6, 7	☐
E2.2b, c, f	List five potential hazards indoors and five potential hazards outdoors. In each case say how you would deal with the hazard.	1, 2, 25	☐
E2.2d, e	What heath and safety hazards are likely if you have animals in the child care setting? How would you minimise them?	1, 21	☐

NVQ UNIT E2

Maintain the safety of children

Element E2.2: Maintain supervision of children

ELEMENT	TASK	REFER TO SPREAD	TASK DONE
E2.2a	The prescribed ratios of adults to children for the age groups below are: • 0–1 years – 1 adult to 3 children • 1–3 years – 1 adult to 4 children • 3–5 years – 1 adult to 8 children Why is it important to have the correct level of supervision?	2, 6	☐
E2.2b	Describe how the adults should behave if there is an emergency or unexpected event.	2, 3, 4	☐
E2.2c	Describe a suitable procedure for collecting children from the care setting. Why is it important to have a set procedure for collecting children? Are there any circumstances when special arrangements might apply to collecting children?	2, 3, 4	☐

NVQ UNIT E2

Maintain the safety of children

Element E2.3: Carry out emergency procedures

ELEMENT	TASK	REFER TO SPREAD	TASK DONE
E2.3a	If an emergency arises which involves evacuating the building: a) What records will you need? b) Why is it important to have accurate records?	2	☐
E2.3b	Describe a routine fire/emergency drill. What are the important actions in a fire drill?	2	☐

NVQ UNIT E2

Maintain the safety of children

Element E2.4: Cope with accident or injuries to children

ELEMENT	TASK	REFER TO SPREAD	TASK DONE
E2.4a	Why is it important not to alarm parents when giving them information about a child's accident or illness?	3, 20	☐
E2.4b, h	Give some examples of reactions of children to accidents. How would you cope with them?	3	☐
E2.4c	List the contents of a First Aid box.	3	☐
E2.4d	What are the priorities when assessing an accident?	3, 4	☐
E2.4e	Describe the First Aid procedure for: a) A child who is unconscious but breathing b) A child who is unconscious and NOT breathing c) A child who has eaten or drunk a poisonous substance d) A child who is choking e) A small cut which is bleeding f) A burn on the hand g) A child who is having a fit h) A nosebleed k) A suspected broken arm	3, 4	☐
E2.4f	Why should accidents be recorded? What details must be recorded?	2, 3, 4	☐
E2.4g	Describe the procedure for handling blood spills. Why is it important to have procedures for handling blood and bodily fluids?	1, 2	☐

NVQ UNIT E2

Maintain the safety of children

Element E2.5: Help keep children safe from abuse

ELEMENT	TASK	REFER TO SPREAD	TASK DONE
E2.5a, d, f	What are the indicators of: • Physical abuse? • Sexual abuse? • Neglect? Why is it important to record and report these? How might these indicators be observed during routine care?	5, 11, 12	☐
E2.5b	Why is it important to follow the stated procedures if abuse is suspected?	5	☐
E2.5c, d	Describe the procedure to be followed by a child care worker if indicators of abuse are observed.	5	☐
E2.5e	Why is it important to involve parents in any enquiries if indicators of abuse are observed?	5	☐

NVQ UNIT E2

Maintain the safety of children

Element E2.6: Ensure children's safety on outings

ELEMENT	TASK	REFER TO SPREAD	TASK DONE
E2.6a	What outings would be suitable for children aged: • 1–2 years • 2–3 years • 3–5 years • 5–7 years	6	☐
E2.6b	From whom do you need to get permission if you are planning to take children on an outing? How would you do this?	6	☐
E2.6c, d,	When planning an outing, what important points do you need to consider with regard to: • Safety? • Transport? • Clothing? • Food? • Equipment? • Insurance?	6	☐
E2.6e	What records and checks will need to be kept while on the outing?	6	☐
E2.6f	In what ways can parents contribute to an outing? What information will parents need about any outing that is being planned?	6	☐

NVQ UNIT P2
Establish and maintain relationships with parents of young children
Element P2.1: Develop relationships with the parents of young children

ELEMENT	TASK	REFER TO SPREAD	TASK DONE
P2.1a	Why is it important for the child care and education setting to have a policy of welcoming parents to share in the care of their children?	41	☐
P2.1b	What information is the parent likely to need from the child care setting?	41, 42	☐
P2.1c	How can you make sure that all parents are included when working in partnership? How can you make sure that information reaches parents whose home language is not the dominant language?	42	☐
P2.1d	Why is confidentiality important? Describe ways in which child care workers can ensure that confidentiality is maintained.	42	☐
P2.1e	What is the major Act of Parliament relating to children?	31, 43	☐

NVQ UNIT P2

Establish and maintain relationships with parents of young children

Element P2.2: Implement settling-in arrangements with parents

ELEMENT	TASK	REFER TO SPREAD	TASK DONE
P2.2a, b, c	What is the likely reaction to separation of: a) A 2-year-old? b) A 6-year-old? Describe a suitable settling-in arrangement for each of these children and their parents. Compare and justify any differences.	35, 41	☐
P2.2d	What policies have to be agreed between parents and the child care setting?	41, 42, 43	☐
P2.2e	What difficulties might be experienced by children and parents whose cultural background is different from the main one in the setting?	30, 31, 39, 41, 42	☐

NVQ UNIT P2

Establish and maintain relationships with parents of young children

Element P2.1: Develop relationships with parents of young children

ELEMENT	TASK	REFER TO SPREAD	TASK DONE
P2.3a	Why is it important to exchange information with parents?	41, 42	☐
P2.3b	What information is needed from parents? How can this information be recorded? (Provide a blank copy of any record forms.) How often should the information be updated?	41, 42	☐
P2.3c	What information will parents need? Give examples of how this information can be made available. Provide an example of an information booklet from a child care setting.	41, 42	☐
P2.3d	How would you arrange for a parent to speak to you privately?	41	☐
P2.3e	Give some examples of barriers to effective communication.	31, 32, 41	☐
P2.3f	Where are confidential records best stored? Who has access to confidential records?	42	☐

NVQ UNIT P2

Establish and maintain relationships with the parents of young children

Element P2.4: Share the care and management of children with their parents

ELEMENT	TASK	REFER TO SPREAD	TASK DONE
P2.4a, b	What are the roles of the child care worker and the parent in the shared care of children? How can child care workers ensure that their care takes account of parents' wishes?	41, 42	☐
P2.4d	Give some examples of how a family's ideas and values may differ from those of the child care setting when managing children's behaviour. How might this be resolved?	31, 32, 41, 42	☐
P2.4c	Describe a suitable procedure for child care workers to follow if a child in their care is ill or has an accident.	20	☐

APPENDIX B
Glossary

ABC of resuscitation   The first actions to be taken when resuscitation is needed. Check airway, breathing and circulation.

Accident book   A method of recording any accident in a child care setting that involves the children or the staff

Admission programme   A systematic plan that is followed to gradually introduce a child to a new setting

Adult/child ratio   The number of adults to children legally required in a child care setting. This is related to the age of the children and the type of setting.

Age-appropriate behaviour   Behaviour that is 'normal' and to be expected at a specific age

Amino acid   The chemical structure of protein

Anaemia   Low haemoglobin levels in the blood linked to iron deficiency in the diet

Antecedent   Something that goes before something else

Anti-discriminatory environment   Physical and social surroundings that encourage a positive view of difference and actively oppose the negative attitudes and practices that lead to unfavourable treatment of people

Associative play   Play involving one child alongside another when they demonstrate some awareness of each other and show signs of communicating with one another

Behaviour modification   A systematic way of changing learned behaviour

Behavioural signs   Observable actions and reactions

Bronchodilator   Drug that causes the airways in the lungs to widen

Carbohydrate   Food that provides energy

Child protection   Procedures aimed at protecting children from all kinds of abuse and giving clear instructions to anyone involved in the care of children if they suspect that a child is at risk of abuse

Child-centred   An approach to learning that takes into account the child's individual capabilities and interests

Children in need   The term used in The Children Act 1989 to describe children for whom a local authority has a duty to provide services

Co-operative play   Play that involves children joining in with other children, often taking on different roles and tasks

Collage   A form of art in which various materials are arranged and glued to a backing

Complete protein   Protein that contains all essential amino acids, usually from animal sources

Conceptual thought   Thought processes that include abstract rather than concrete ideas

Confidentiality Keeping sensitive and personal information secret from anyone who does not have a right to have access to it

Creative play Play that involves children expressing their own ideas through a variety of media, including paint and music

Cross-infection The passing of an infection from one person to another

Dehydration Insufficient fluid intake to maintain fluid balance in the body

Department of Social Security The central government department that distributes financial and other benefits

Designated person The person in a child care setting who is responsible for child protection procedures and to whom any suspicions of child abuse should first be reported

Discrimination and discriminatory practices Unfavourable treatment of a person based on prejudice and negative attitudes

Display techniques Ways of presenting two- and three-dimensional work on walls or other areas so that they can be explored via the senses

Droplet infection Pathogens contained in the droplets of water in the breath which are passed on to others

'E' number Number given to permitted food additives

Egocentric Self-centred ideas or actions

Emergency procedure Sequence of priorities for assisting a child at risk

Emotional abuse Action which harms a child's developing feelings

Emotional maturity The ability to express and control a variety of feelings in an age-appropriate manner; a level of emotional development that is appropriate or more characteristic of someone at an older age

Empowerment Enabling of people with disabilities to take part in the world effectively and on their own terms

Enzyme deficiency A lack of a particular enzyme so that the chemical reaction it performs in the body is not carried out

Equality of opportunity Enabling all people to have an equal chance of participating in life to the best of their abilities

Ethnic group A group of people who share a distinctive culture

Family diversity The different forms that families can take, including differences in structure, size and culture

Fat-soluble vitamin Vitamin that can be stored in the body

Fever A temperature above 37°C (37°C is a normal temperature)

Fine motor The use of the hands and fingers to manipulate objects

First Aid Immediate treatment given at the scene of an accident or sudden illness

Food additive A substance added to foods labelled with an 'E' number

Food intolerance An unusual reaction to a particular food

Foreign body An unusual object lodged in the body, e.g. a splinter

Framework for children's behaviour The goals and boundaries that adults set for children's behaviour

Gluten A protein found in wheat, barley, oats and rye

Goals and boundaries Goals are the behaviour that adults decide they want children to aim for; boundaries are the outer limits of what is deemed acceptable behaviour

Grief The intensely sad feelings caused by the loss of a person or thing to whom one has an attachment

Gross motor The movement and posture of the arms, legs and body

Hand/eye co-ordination The hands and eyes working together to enable the hands to perform increasingly delicate tasks

HIB Haemophilus influenza type B immunisation; protects against meningitis

Hygiene routines Regular procedures which aim to promote children's health and physical well being.

Imaginative play Play that involves children forming mental images of objects or people not present, or using one object to represent another

Imitative play Play that involves children copying someone or something that they have seen

Immunisation The use of vaccine to protect people from disease

Impairment A limitation to the way that a part of the body works

Incomplete protein Protein foods which by themselves do not supply all the essential amino acids

Independence Not depending on another person to perform a task or to achieve a goal

Indicator of neglect Sign that a child's physical needs are not being provided for

Institutionalised discrimination Unfavourable treatment of people built into the systems and processes of an organisation

Insulin A hormone produced by the pancreas which is essential for carbohydrate metabolism

Interaction Two-way communication between people

Interest table Display of objects on a table, usually around a theme, that helps children to understand their environment through examining the objects

Intervention Changing the course of events by coming either between two people, or a person and an object, or a person and an activity

Koplik's spots Spots which can be seen in the mouth in the early stages of measles

Language diversity The existence of different languages, accents, dialects or other ways of communicating in one environment

Legal and political framework Laws and political system within which services are provided

Local Authority The elected body that is responsible for the provision of local services in an area

Malleable materials Substances that can be moulded into different shapes without cracking or breaking

Manipulative play Play that involves using the hands to achieve a goal

Mineral An essential part of diet absorbed from the soil by vegetables, cereals and fruit

Monitoring Regularly checking and assessing the results of observations

Multicultural society A social community that includes members from a variety of different cultural backgrounds

Multiple transitions The experience by a child of continual changes of carers and care environments

National Curriculum The compulsory subjects that children must study in state schools, introduced as part of the 1988 Education Reform Act

National Health Service The provision of free health care by the state, introduced following the Second World War. Charging has now been introduced for some services.

Natural and manufactured materials Substances produced by nature and those that are man-made

Non-verbal communication Conveying meaning without the use of words

Observation Accurately watching and taking notice

Otitis media An infection of the middle ear

Painful crisis Term used to describe the pain and other symptoms produced by Sickle Cell disease

Palmar grasp Using the whole of the hand and fingers to purposefully grasp an object

Parallel play Children playing alongside each other with an awareness of each others' existence but not co-operating

Parasites Harmful organisms which invade humans and depend on them for food, such as headlice

Parental involvement The inclusion of parents in different aspects of the care and education of their children within institutions

Partnership with parents Positive relationship between educators/carers and parents, involving the open exchange of information. The idea is one of the principles of The Children Act 1989.

Pathogen Harmful organisms which invade the body, e.g. bacteria and viruses; commonly called germs

Personal hygiene Keeping the body clean and well cared for

Physical abuse Deliberately hurting or harming a child

Piaget An influential psychologist who looked at the role of play in the development of children's thinking and understanding

Pincer grasp Using the thumb and forefinger to pick up objects

Potential hazard A danger to children which can be foreseen and prevented by good practice

Prejudice Negative attitudes based on incomplete information and stereotypical assumptions

Preventive health Measures which can be taken to avoid illness

Private services Services that are provided in order to meet a demand. They involve the charging of fees with the aim of making a profit for the providers.

Racism Negative attitudes and beliefs of superiority expressed by a dominant racial group in a variety of ways towards people of another racial group

Recovery position Safe lying-down posture allowing an unconscious casualty to keep the airway open

Regression Going back to an earlier stage of development; often a temporary occurrence associated with a stressful situation in a child's life

Rickets A condition where the bones fail to harden, usually associated with a lack of vitamin D

Role model Someone who provides an example of behaviour that is likely to be copied by another person as a pattern for their own behaviour

Role play Play that involves children pretending to be a different person in a particular role, e.g. playing 'mummy'

Safe environment A place where all reasonable steps are taken to minimise potential hazards to children's safety

Saturated fat Fats which are solid at room temperature and come mainly from animal sources

Screening Programmes undertaken to review a child's developmental progress and to detect specific problems

Self-image, self-identity, self-esteem The idea or picture that a person has of themselves, and how well or badly they think of themselves (i.e. high or low self-esteem)

Sensory Motor stage The stage of intellectual development typical of children 0–2 years old, during which they explore and manipulate their environment to see how they can affect it

Social Services Department The local government department that implements Acts of Parliament concerning the care and protection of vulnerable people in society, often with the help of social workers

Social skills Aids to independence and meeting particular cultural requirements

Solitary play A child playing alone without taking notice of others who may be near

Spread of infection Transmission of disease via direct and indirect spread

Statutory services Services which local or central government has a power or a duty to provide, as a result of the passing of laws

Stereotypical assumptions Believing something without proof and basing those beliefs on generalised ideas, not on facts

Symbolic play Play that involves a child letting an object stand for (or symbolise) something else, e.g. a box becomes a car. Usually begins at around two years.

The Children Act 1989 Comprehensive piece of child care legislation, bringing together previous public and private laws with the aim of protecting children in any situation. Came into effect in October 1991.

Theories Ideas or general principles that try to explain why things happen in the way that they do

Toilet training Teaching children bowel and bladder control and the use of toilet or potty

Transition Movement of a child from one care situation to another

Tripod grasp Use of thumb and two fingers to grasp an object

Unsaturated fat Fats which are liquid at room temperature and come mainly from vegetable sources

Values and norms The beliefs, customs and rules that underpin the behaviour of individuals and groups

Vegan A diet that excludes eating any animal products

Voluntary organisations Groups providing services based on a perception of need, but not for profit or because of a statutory obligation

Water-soluble vitamin A vitamin that cannot be stored by the body

Waterborne infection An infection spread by drinking infected water or eating food washed in infected water

Welfare State The combination of services provided by the state for all citizens, based on legislation passed in the 1940s, with the aim of protecting their health, providing financial resources and education from birth to death (or 'from the cradle to the grave')

Workplace policies and procedures A set of rules used by all child care workers in a work place to ensure a uniform response to a particular situation

APPENDIX C
Further Reading

BAECE: *Play: The Key To Young Children's Learning* (British Association for Early Childhood Education, 1996)

Beaver, M, Brewster, J, Jones, P, Keene, A, Neaum, S, Tallack J: *Babies And Young Children*, Book 1: *Development*, Book 2: *Work and Care* (Stanley Thornes, 1995)

British Red Cross: *First Aid For Children* (Dorling Kindersley, 1994)

Dare, A, O'Donovan, M: *A Practical Guide To Child Nutrition* (Stanley Thornes, 1996)

Davenport, G: *An Introduction To Child Development*, second edition (Collins Educational, 1994)

HMSO: *An Introduction To The Children Act* (HMSO, 1989)

Hobart, C, Frankel, J: *A Practical Guide To Working With Young Children* (Stanley Thornes, 1996)

Hobart, C, Frankel, J: *A Practical Guide To Activities For Young Children* (Stanley Thornes, 1996)

Lindon, J: *Child Development From Birth To Eight – A Practical Focus* (National Children's Bureau, 1993)

Moore, S: *Sociology Alive* (Stanley Thornes, 1987)

Moyles, J: *Just Playing? The Role And Status Of Play In Early Childhood Education* (Open University Press, 1989)

Open College: *Working With Young Children* series (Open College, 1994)

Tallack, J, Neaum, S: *Good Practice In Implementing The Pre-School Curriculum* (Stanley Thornes, 1997)

APPENDIX D
Multiple Choice Answers

Answers to Paper 1

1	d	11	b	21	b	31	b
2	b	12	b	22	d	32	b
3	a	13	c	23	a	33	b
4	b	14	c	24	a	34	d
5	b	15	b	25	c	35	a
6	d	16	c	26	c	36	c
7	b	17	c	27	c	37	c
8	b	18	b	28	a	38	b
9	c	19	a	29	a	39	b
10	b	20	b	30	a	40	d

Answers to Paper 2

1	c	11	b	21	d	31	a
2	d	12	b	22	b	32	c
3	d	13	d	23	d	33	c
4	d	14	c	24	a	34	d
5	c	15	b	25	a	35	a
6	b	16	b	26	b	36	b
7	b	17	b	27	a	37	b
8	d	18	d	28	b	38	d
9	d	19	b	29	b	39	a
10	a	20	d	30	b	40	b

Answers to Paper 3

1	b	11	a	21	c	31	d
2	c	12	c	22	d	32	d
3	b	13	a	23	d	33	b
4	b	14	d	24	d	34	d
5	a	15	a	25	c	35	a
6	b	16	b	26	c	36	b
7	c	17	b	27	c	37	c
8	b	18	d	28	c	38	d
9	b	19	a	29	c	39	a
10	b	20	a	30	d	40	b

INDEX

ABC of resuscitation 6
accident book 5
accidents 4
admissions 89
adult role 52, 53
allergy 38
amino acid 26
anaemia 28,29
antecedent 78, 79
antibiotics 39
assessment 78
assignment 101–110
asthma 7, 38
athlete's foot 35

bacteria 34
behaviour 78, 79, 82,
   83, 84, 85
behaviour modifi-
   cation 84
behavioural signs 10
benefits of exercise 15
bibliography 108,115
bilingual 68
bleeding 6
books 49, 54, 55, 69
boundaries 83
broncho-dilator 38
burns 6

CACHE 101
calcium 29
carbohydrates 26, 27
caring for a sick child
   40–41
causes of disease 34

CCE 116–119
chickenpox 35,36
child abuse 10,11
child protection 10,11
childhood illness
   34–41
Children Act 1989,
   69, 91, 93
choking 6
Christians 30
climbing 17
clothing 23
Coeliac disease 31, 38
colds 35, 36
collage 58
comforters 48
communication 51, 54
   with parents 88, 89
conclusion 108
conflict with parents
   87
cooking 57
coughs 35, 36
creativity 58
cross-referencing 118
cross-infection 2
cultural diversity 55,
   57, 68
cystic fibrosis 31, 39

dehydration 36, 40
democracy 90
dental decay 28
designated person 11
development 51, 54,
   57, 61, 70, 72, 73,

75
diabetes 7, 31, 39
diarrhoea 35, 36
diary 118
diet 26–33
dietary principles 30
diphtheria 2 31,36
disability 45, 49,
   64–67, 69
discrimination 63–66,
   69
display 46, 47
dressing 25
droplet infection 35

'E' numbers 32
ear infection 36
eating 25
emergency procedures
   5
emotional abuse 10
emotional devel-
   opment 31
empowerment 65
endorsements 113
environment 44–45
enzymes 39
equal opportunities
   104
equality of oppor-
   tunity 66, 67, 69
equipment 23, 44, 49

fat-soluble vitamin 27
fats 27, 28
fever 40